Giant Book of
WINNING
SCIENCE FAIR
PROJECTS

Bob Bonnet
& Dan Keene

A Main Street Book

10 9 8 7 6 5 4 3 2 1

Published In 2000 by Sterling Publishing Company, Inc.
387 Park Avenue South, New York, N.Y. 10016

Material in this collection was adapted from
Science Fair Projects: The Environment
© 1995 by Bob Bonnet and Dan Keene
Science Fair Projects: Energy
© 1997 by Bob Bonnet and Dan Keene
and
Science Fair Projects: Flight, Space, and Astronomy
© 1997 by Bob Bonnet and Dan Keene

Distributed in Canada by Sterling Publishing
c/o Canadian Manda Group
One Atlantic Avenue, Suite 105
Toronto, Ontario, Canada M6K 3E7
Distributed in Great Britain and Europe by Cassell PLC
Wellington House, 125 Strand
London WC2R 0BB, United Kingdom
Distributed in Australia by Capricorn Link (Australia) Pty Ltd.
P.O. Box 6651, Baulkham Hills, Business Centre,
NSW 2153, Australia

Sterling ISBN 0-8069-4341-6

CONTENTS

SCIENCE FAIR PROJECTS

The material in this book is presented in a light and interesting fashion. For example, the concept of measurement can be demonstrated by teaching precise measuring in inches or centimeters (equivalents in this book are approximate), or by having a child stretch his or her arms around a tree trunk and asking, "Are all children's reaches the same?" We present science in a way that does not seem like science.

The scientific concepts introduced here will help the young student to understand more advanced scientific principles later. Projects will develop those science skills needed in our ever-increasing complex society: skills such as classifying objects, making measured observations, thinking clearly ,and recording data accurately. Values are dealt with in a general way. One should never harm any living thing just for the sake of it. Respect for life should be fundamental. Disruption of natural processes should not occur thoughtlessly and unnecessarily. Interference with ecological systems should always be avoided.

The activities presented in this book target third- through fifth-grade students. The materials needed to do most of the activities are commonly found around the home or are easily available at minimal cost.

Because safety is and must always be the first consideration, we recommend that all activities be done under adult supervision. Even seemingly harmless objects can become a hazard under certain circumstances. For example, a bowling ball can be a danger if it is allowed to fall on a child's foot.

There are many benefits in store for a child who chooses to do a science project. It motivates the child to learn. Such an activity helps develop thinking skills; it prompts a child to question, and learn how to solve problems.

In these activities, the child is asked to make observations using all the senses and to record those observations accurately and honestly. Quantitative measurements of distance, size, and volume must be made. Students may find a subject so interesting that, after the project is completed, they will want to do more investigation on their own. Spin-off interests can develop, too. In doing a science project about energy conservation, while using a computer to record data, a child may discover an interest in computers.

The authors recommend that parents take an active interest in their child's science project. Apart from the safety aspect, when a parent is involved, contact time between the parent and child increases. Such quality time strengthens relationships as well as the child's self-esteem. Working on a project is an experience that can be shared. An involved parent is telling the child that he or she believes that education is important. Parents need to support the academic learning process at least as much as they support Little League, music lessons, or any other growth activity

Parents should take the time to help the student in reading, understanding, and completing these educational and fun projects. Adults can be an invaluable resource that the child draws upon for information, as older people are given the opportunity to share their own learning and life experiences. Transportation may be helpful and appreciated, such as taking the child to a library or other places for research. One student in our school, doing a project on insects, was taken by his parents to the Mosquito Commission Laboratory, where he was able to talk with professionals in the field.

Many projects in this book have been designed as "around-you science," in contrast to "book science." By "around-you science" we mean doing a science project right where you are—in your home, your neighborhood, your school. Getting ideas for a science fair project can even begin right at your feet. What happens when you kick a rock? Why are darker colors worn in the wintertime? Is there energy in your body? How did it get there? What can you do to save energy in your home or or school? Get excited with your child about the world around us!

Clear and creative thought is a primary goal for the young scientific mind. This book will help prepare a young person for future involvement and satisfying experiences in the field of science.

ENERGY

A Note to the Parent

All children are scientists, constantly searching for explanations to their questions about the world around them. Their quest should be enjoyable, interesting, and thought-provoking…as science is. This is the concept that the writers wish to convey in this book. In addition to presenting many valuable and useful scientific ideas and learning techniques, the book is designed to entice the young child with the excitement and fun of scientific investigation.

ENERGY

Welcome to the fascinating world of energy! This book explores projects in energy and the physics of energy. The term "energy" is difficult to give a meaning to, since it is found in many forms and is closely linked to "forces" (magnetism, gravity, wind, etc.). Physicists define energy as the ability to do work, and they define "work" as the ability to move an object over a distance.

Forms of energy include solar, mechanical, chemical, electrical, moving fluids (both gases and liquids, etc.), heat, light, sound, pressure, thermal, nuclear, electromagnetic waves, respiration (living things get energy from foods, and muscles do work), and the forces of weather, gravity, and magnetism.

Energy can be transferred from one object to another; a rolling marble strikes a stationary marble and causes it to start rolling. Energy can be converted from one form to another, such as light energy to heat energy. Albert Einstein is known for the formula $E = mc2$ he put forth in 1905, stating that matter can be changed into energy and energy into matter.

Energy is said to be either "kinetic" or "potential." Potential energy is "stored-up" energy—something that has the ability to do work. Kinetic energy is the energy of movement, when work is actually being done. Potential energy can be converted into kinetic energy, and vice versa. Energy from sunlight is stored in trees (potential energy), which can be burned in a fireplace to produce heat (kinetic energy). Roll a rock up a hill (using kinetic energy), and set it on the hilltop (potential energy), where, because of gravity, it has the potential to do work (when it falls).

Project 1
SHRINKING CUBES
Changing the sun's light into heat energy

Imagine a sunny day at a picnic. You pour a glass of cola soda to drink. Your friend fills a glass with a lemon-lime soda he likes. You both take one ice cube. Which ice cube will last longer?

Sunlight turns into heat energy. Things that are dark in color absorb more light energy than those that are lighter, so they become hotter. Will the darker soda collect more sunlight and melt the cube faster?

Take two same-size clear glasses, fill one with a clear or light-colored soda and one with a dark-colored drink. Fill each glass to the same height, not quite to the top. Place the glasses in a sunny window for a half hour. Then, take two ice cubes of equal size and drop one into each glass. Which of the two ice cubes lasts longer? Why?

You need
- 2 same-size clear drinking glasses
- clear-colored soda drink
- dark-colored soda drink
- a table by a sunny window
- 2 same-size ice cubes
- a dark room

In this project, an assumption is made. We are assuming (we "think") that the kind of soda itself (flavor, sweetness) does not affect the melting of the ice cubes. To prove that our assumption is correct, do the experiment again. This time, set both glasses of soda in a dark room instead of in the sun. If both ice cubes take the same amount of time to melt, then the sodas had an equal effect on the ice cubes, and our assumption is correct Test out other drinks: orange juice, red punch, lemonade, ginger ale. Try carbonated/noncarbonated, diet (sugar substitute)/high sugar, with/without solids (pulp), etc.

What else about a drink might affect the melting speed of ice cubes? How can you find out if it does?

9

Project 2
FROSTY'S SUNSCREEN
Warding off the sun's heating rays

It's fun to build a snowman and have it stand guard in your yard all winter long. But rising temperatures and the sun's heat are not kind to snowmen. It can quickly make them melt away.

Will putting a "hat" or kerchief on your snowman's head help shade him from the sun and keep him around longer?

On a sunny day when there is snow on the ground, build two identical snowmen. Fold a large black plastic (trash) bag into a kerchief or hat and place or tie it on the head of one snowman. You might need to use snow or small twigs to help hold it in place.

Fold a large white plastic bag as you did the black and place it on the head of the other snowman. Again, keep it in place by tying or using snow or small twigs.

As the day goes by, check each snowman to see if there has been any melting. If so, which one's head shows the most melting?

Plastic bags often come in other colors—blue, red, and green, for example. Would using these colors as hats make any difference in keeping a snowman around longer? Would using no kerchief make a difference? (If there's not enough snow available to make several large, whole snowmen, just make large snowball "heads" and wrap same-size sections of the different-colored bags on them for this experiment.)

> **You need**
> - a sunny day with snow on the ground
> - large black plastic bag
> - large white plastic bag

10

Project 3
GETTING STEAMED
Water vapor put to work

Steam is water changed into a gas by heat energy. We use the energy of steam to do many things. Steam has been used to power boats and trains. Steam turbines generate electricity when steam pressure pushes against blades or paddles connected to a shaft and turns the shaft. On the other end of the shaft is an electrical generator.

Get a Pyrex beaker, a one-hole rubber stopper, and a glass tube with a 90-degree, or right-angle, bend. These items can be purchased inexpensively at a science store or borrowed from your science teacher at school.

Never work around a hot stove without an adult with you. Be very careful! The stove burner, the beaker, and the escaping steam will be hot. Do not touch them!

Pour some water into the beaker. Insert the rubber stopper in the top; then ask an adult to gently push one end of the bent glass tube through the hole in the stopper.

Set the beaker on the burner of a stove or a hot plate and turn it on high heat. Open the pages slightly of a tall hard-bound book and stand it next to (but not too close to) the burner. Lay a toy pinwheel on a stick on top of the book and extend it out so that the pinwheel paddles are in the path of the escaping steam from the tube. Do you think heat energy is being changed into mechanical energy?

> ### You need
> - an adult
> - toy pinwheel
> - Pyrex beaker
> - stove burner or hot plate
> - one-hole rubber stopper
> - glass tube with a 90° bend

Project 4
HOT STUFF
Heat energy from decomposition

Heat energy is given off when organic things (material that was once alive) decay. Many people who plant gardens have "compost piles" to make fertilizer for feeding the garden. A compost pile is a small area, often boxed, filled with dead or dying plant and animal leavings such as peels and scraps from the kitchen, fallen leaves, grass clippings, manure, hay, and other things that rot. The material is stacked and allowed to decay for months, as it turns into rich fertilizer. As it decays, heat is given off.

You need
- freshly mowed grass clippings
- a warm, sunny day
- lawn rake
- clock or watch

When your lawn or your neighbor's lawn is mowed, gather some grass clippings by using a lawn rake. Make a pile of grass clippings 1 foot (30 cm) high and about 1 foot (30 cm) in diameter. Place the pile on the lawn in a bright, sunny spot. Let it sit in the sunlight.

After two hours, use the rake to make another pile of grass clippings and place it next to the first one. Both piles should be the same size. Wait ten minutes. Then push one hand into the middle of each pile. Does the inside of one pile feel warmer than the other? If so, which pile feels warmer, the one you just raked or the one that has been sitting in the sunlight for two hours?

Do you think grass clippings can be used to make a good habitat or nest for some animals?

Project 5
BOTTLED GAS
Stored chemical energy (CO$_2$) in soda

Carbon dioxide (CO$_2$) is a colorless gas. Humans and animals breathe out carbon dioxide. It is also formed when things made of carbon, such as charcoal, wood, and coal, are burned.

You need
- balloon
- bottle of carbonated soda

Energy is used by the food industry to dissolve carbon dioxide into water; this adds the "fizz" to carbonated soda drinks. As long as the soda bottle remains unopened or the opened soda is kept tightly capped, the carbon dioxide stays dissolved. But as soon as the cap is taken off the bottle, the carbon dioxide starts to expand and escape (this is chemical energy).

What happens when you pour a carbonated soda into a glass slowly? What happens when you pour fast? The release of carbon dioxide is what makes the bubbles in soda, and gives it a foamy head. We can show that there is energy being released by making the expanding carbon dioxide do work. First, stretch a balloon several times in all directions. Blow it up as big as it will go, then let all the air out. Doing this will make the balloon easier to inflate.

Open a bottle of carbonated soda (read the label if you aren't sure whether the drink is carbonated). Remove the cap and stretch the opening of the balloon over the mouth of the bottle. Carefully, shake the bottle to release carbon dioxide from the soda. What happens to the balloon?

Do you have an unopened bottle of soda that has been stored for a long time? Put the balloon over its mouth when you do open it. Does the balloon inflate? What does that tell you about the CO$_2$ in the soda, and the plastic container or tightness of its cap?

Project 6
ROLLING STOCK
Potential energy, mass, and gravity

Energy used to move an object up to a height is stored in the object as "potential energy" because gravity pulls downward on the object and will cause it to move. If two objects are raised to the same height, which has more energy stored in it (required more energy to move), the lighter object (less mass) or the heavier one (more mass)?

Stack several books on the floor, making two piles the same height, about 1 foot (30 cm) tall. Make two ramps by propping one end of each long board up on a stack. Shelf boards work well if you have them; if not, have an adult help you find two same-size boards, or cut two boards from a section of plywood.

Fill a plastic two-liter soda bottle with water and screw the cap on tightly. Screw the cap onto another, empty, plastic two-liter soda bottle. Lift both bottles to the top of the ramps, laying them on their sides, and hold them. Then let go of both of them at the same time. Which one travels farther? The one that travels farther had more potential energy, and therefore also took more energy to move to the top of the ramp.

The bottle that travels farther also has more "momentum." Momentum is a force that moves an object. It is the product of mass times velocity. The bottle filled with water has more mass than the empty one. Now, why do you think it is hard to stop a moving train quickly?

A ramp is an "inclined plane," a type of simple machine. Research inclined planes.

> **You need**
> - 2 two-liter plastic soda bottles
> - books
> - ruler
> - 2 boards, about 1 by 4 feet (30 by120 cm)
> - water
> - an adult

Project 7
STORMY WEATHER
Detecting the energy release of storms

Tremendous amounts of energy are released every minute around the world by the Earth's weather system. Lightning,, wind, hurricanes, and tornadoes are powerful energy producers. It is said that lightning strikes somewhere on Earth 100 times each second! A lightning

> **You need**
> - a storm
> - pencil and paper
> - AM radio

bolt is thought to release as much as 100 million volts of electricity, and reach a temperature as high as 50,000 degrees Fahrenheit (27,760 Celsius).

Next time it storms, look out your windows.* Make a list of evidence that energy is being released by the storm. Remember, energy "works" (the ability to move something over a distance). So, what do you see: trees moving, leaves stirring, the flag and rope on a flagpole whipping around, sand blowing, a clothes line jiggling, a can rolling noisily down the street, paper flying through the air? Is smoke from chimneys rising straight up, or bending or scattering? Are there fierce-looking waves on a large nearby lake? Is sea water spraying from the tops of rough ocean waves?

If it is raining, is the rain falling straight down or at an angle? What is happening when the rain hits the ground? Is a heavy rain causing streams down streets and across yards? Is there evidence of erosion—soil being pushed by the moving water?Open a window a bit and listen. Write down the sounds of energy release. Do you hear the wailing of the wind? If it is a thunderstorm, do you see lightning and hear the crash of thunder that follows? Using your AM radio, can you detect the crackle and static of radio frequency energy released by the lightning?

*Storms can be dangerous. Make your observations from the safety and comfort of your home. If lightning is *nearby*, do not use the telephone, and move away from windows.

Project 8
BRICK TRICK
Transfer of heat energy in a solid

Heat energy can be transferred, or move *through* an object or *from* one object to another.

Lay two empty small-size (pint) milk cartons on their side, with the spout openings facing upward. With scissors, carefully cut the top side off each carton. The cartons will serve as molds to make two bricks.

First, using the cartons as measuring containers, fill one and a half pint cartons with sand and pour it into an old bucket or paint can. Add 6 ounces of liquid white glue and 2 ounces of water. Mix thoroughly. Then spoon the mixture into an old shirt or a large piece of cheesecloth, and squeeze out any excess water.

Place the mixture into each milk-carton mold. In each one, push a pencil halfway into the brick, near one end, and leave it there.

Place the bricks in a sunny window for a few days, until they harden. Roll the pencils that are in the bricks between your fingers a few times as the bricks dry, so the pencils will be easier to remove later. When the bricks

You need
- 2 small-size milk cartons
- an old bucket or paint can
- an old shirt or cheesecloth
- sand
- water
- liquid white glue
- a tablespoon or scoop
- 2 pencils
- 2 thermometers
- cardboard, about 1 foot (30 cm) square
- scissors
- a sunny window
- wooden paint stirrer or other stick
- paper
- clock or watch

are dry and hard, take the pencils out of the bricks. Put a thermometer in each hole left by the pencils.

In a room that has a sunny window, place one brick near the window, where it can get sunlight. Position it so that the end that has the thermometer stuck in it is away from the window. Cut a piece of cardboard to fit over the brick, making a sunshield, so that the front half of the brick is in sunlight but the back half is in shade. Place the other brick on a table in the same room, but away from the sunlight.

Read and write down the temperatures showing on both thermometers. Every five minutes, read and write down the temperatures again. After one hour, compare the temperatures you recorded for both bricks. Did the one in the sunny window show a warmer temperature? Did heat from the sunny side of the brick travel through the brick to the other end? What was the "rate of heat transfer," that is, how fast did the heat move through the brick (one degree every five minutes, two degrees every five minutes, *three* degrees every five minutes…)?

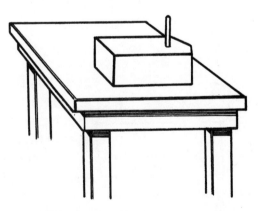

Project 9
SAILS ALOFT
Using wind energy to power a boat

From mankind's early days, sails have been used on boats to harness the energy of the wind. Let's make small sailboats, using quart-size milk cartons, and experiment with different shapes and sizes of sails.

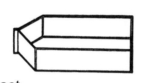

Lay an empty quart milk carton on its side, with the spout-opening upward. With scissors, cut off the top half of the carton lengthwise to make a boat.

Near the front (pointed end), place a small mound of modeling clay. To make a mast, push the eraser end of a pencil into the clay. A small amount of clay may be needed near the back of the boat to keep the boat balanced. Tape a 1-foot-long (30 cm) piece of string onto the back of the boat so it will drag in the water (this will help hold the boat on course).

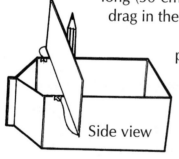

Side view

Cut a sail out of a piece of paper and tape it to the pencil mast. You may need tape or thread to hold the bottom ends of the paper to the sides of the boat, keeping the sail tight in strong winds. Make several boats using sails of different sizes and shapes.

Find a place outdoors—a small lake, shallow pond, wading pool, public fountain—where you can sail your boat. Have an adult with you for safety around water. Which sail design do you think will make the boats go fastest? Test your sail design.

At the library, research "sailboats" and try different designs on your boats.

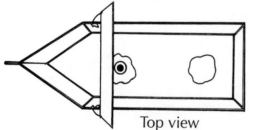

Top view

You need
- stiff paper
- thread
- pencils
- modeling clay
- string
- scissors
- quart milk cartons
- adhesive tape
- body of shallow water
- an adult

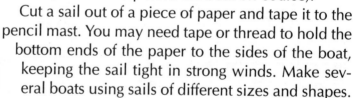

Project 10
SALT OR NOT?
Comparing solar energy storage in salt and fresh water

Compared to air, water is slow to change temperature. If the weather has been hot for a few days and the water in a swimming pool is warm, one night of cooler temperatures will not change the temperature in the pool very much. It will still be almost as warm the next day.

Does the ability of water to hold the heat energy it has collected differ if the water is salt water or fresh water? Does a saltwater lake cool differently than a freshwater lake when the sun sets?

Fill two 2-liter soda bottles with equally hot water from your kitchen sink (let it run a bit until you get a constant temperature). Add eight teaspoons of salt to one bottle. Stir to dissolve the salt thoroughly.

Instead of screwing the caps on, lightly place a ball of modeling clay over the mouth of each bottle. Carefully push a thermometer into the bottle alongside the clay, so that the bulb of the thermometer is in the water. Make sure you can read the temperature on the thermometer, then press the clay against the thermometer to hold it in place. Do this to both bottles.

Every ten minutes, read the thermometers and write down the temperature readings. After two hours, compare the temperatures you recorded. Did they both lose heat energy at the same rate?

> **You need**
> - salt
> - 2 two-liter soda bottles
> - 2 thermometers
> - modeling clay
> - hot tap water
> - clock
> - paper and pencil

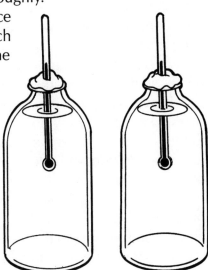

Project 11
THINGS ARE HEATING UP
Graphing solar energy collection in materials

As the sun beats down on the Earth, heat energy is absorbed by everything on the surface. What gathers more of the sun's heat energy: air, water, sand, or stone?

Find four large glasses or, using scissors, carefully cut the top half off four clear 2-liter plastic bottles. (Place the discarded tops in a recyclables trash container.) Stand a ruler upright on a table alongside the container (glass or bottle bottom). Four inches (10 cm) above the table surface, mark the container using a small strip of adhesive tape. Place the top of the tape at the 4-inch height. Do this for all four containers, then write the contents of each container on the tape (air, water, sand or soil, stones). The tape will serve as both a label and the fill-to mark for the containers.

Leave one container empty ("filled" with air). Fill another to the 4-inch mark with water. Fill a third up to the mark with sandy soil. The bulb of each thermometer must be placed, hanging, in the middle of each container, not touching the sides or bottom. For the containers of air and water, suspend the thermometers by placing a section of tape at the top of the thermometer and over a pencil or stick placed across the top of a container. The thermometer bulb should be hanging about 2 inches (5 cm) from the bottom of the container. Carefully push a thermometer down partway into the sandy soil. For the fourth container, hold a thermometer inside the container with one hand so

You need
- scissors
- 4 large glasses (or empty 2-liter bottle bottoms)
- a sunny window
- ruler
- masking tape
- water
- sandy soil
- small stones
- 4 thermometers
- 2 pencils or sticks
- clock
- paper and pencil

that the bulb is 2 inches (5 cm) below the fill line. With the other hand, gently place small stones, about fi to 1 inch (1–2.5 cm) in diameter, up to the container's fill line.

Set the four containers in a sunny window. After one hour, measure the temperature of each material by reading the thermometers. Write down the temperature readings and compare them.

Take all four containers out of the sunny window and place them somewhere in the room that is out of direct sunlight. Every five minutes for thirty minutes, read the temperatures on the thermometers and write them down in a list. Thirty minutes later, after an hour has passed, record the final temperature readings. Which container lost heat the fastest? Which material continued to give off heat the longest? Was this also the same material that gathered the most heat?

For your project display, make up four simple graphs, see sample for Air. Across the top (X-axis) put in the time of the readings (every 5 minutes). List temperatures going down the chart (Y-axis). Then enter your own time–temperature readings of each tested material on its chart.

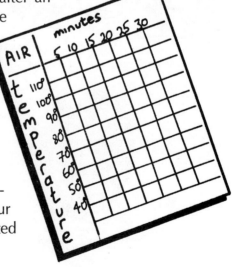

Project 12
WANT, HELP, NEED
Categorizing home electrical appliances

Many appliances in our homes or apartments save us work and make our lives healthier, hap-

You need
• paper and pencil

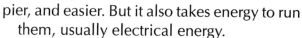

pier, and easier. But it also takes energy to run them, usually electrical energy.

Making up a list, search through each room of your home and look for things that use electrical energy (the refrigerator in the kitchen, a hair dryer in the bedroom, lamps in the den, a TV set in the living room). Be sure to include such things as smoke alarms, flashlights, and portable radios, which work off electrical energy stored in batteries.

Once your list is complete, think about each item on your list, and decide if that energy-user is a want (you like and want it), a help (makes your life easier), or a need (necessary in your household).

A need is something that you really must have in order to have a healthy, safe, and working home. If your home is not connected to your city's water system, you probably have a well. In that case, an electric water pump would be necessary to you, supplying water for cooking, cleaning, washing, and personal hygiene.

Consider a help to be something in your home that it is good to have, but that you could do without if you had to. A flashlight would be something you would put in the help category. It's handy to have one in your home in case there is an electric power failure, which might happen during a storm, but day to day you could live without it.

A want is something we have in our home simply because we like it. Usually its purpose is to make our life more enjoyable. A video game may be very entertaining, but it is not necessary to our health or survival.

Some items may fall under a different category for different homes. Although a telephone answering machine is usually just a convenience (a want), if someone is running a business in the home an answering machine may be more of a help or even a necessity, or important business calls could be lost.

Don't forget to check outside your home, too. See if there are any energy-using devices in your yard, such as a swimming-pool pump or security lighting, that should be added to your list.

Project 13
YESTERDAY'S ENERGY
Conserving fossil fuels

Fossil fuels are sources of energy that we find within the Earth. We release the energy from such fuels as oil, coal, and natural gas by burning them. These fossil fuels are the re-

You need
• pencil and paper

mains of animal life and vegetation (energy in the form of trapped sunlight) that have been within the Earth for millions of years. At the current rate, we are using up our resources of fossil fuels faster than the Earth can make more. Unless we use these fuels more wisely, we will someday run out.

Is your home heated by the burning of fossil fuels? You can save natural gas or heating oil by not letting heat escape through open or drafty doors or windows in cold weather. Can you reduce the need for heating by trapping some of the sun's warming solar energy indoors?

The gasoline that cars run on is made from fossil fuels, so automobile manufacturers are always working to make their cars more fuel-efficient. By driving more slowly and not using cars as much when they don't need to, car owners can help conserve gasoline, too. How else can we help save fossil fuels? Many electrical power plants make electricity by burning fossil fuels.

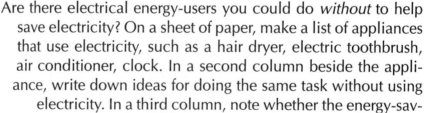

Are there electrical energy-users you could do *without* to help save electricity? On a sheet of paper, make a list of appliances that use electricity, such as a hair dryer, electric toothbrush, air conditioner, clock. In a second column beside the appliance, write down ideas for doing the same task without using electricity. In a third column, note whether the energy-saving way would be "a little inconvenient," "very inconvenient," or "a real hardship."

Are there other things to consider about energy usage? You might think of replacing a 100-watt bulb with a 60-watt bulb to save energy. But if the bulb lights the cellar stairway, would it be bright enough to make going down the stairway safe?

Project 14
ONE IF BY LAND
Comparing land and water solar-heat storage

The sun warms our planet. As the Earth turns and night falls, the surface the sun has warmed begins to cool, radiating the heat energy absorbed during the day. What loses heat faster—a body of water or the land near it?

Find a lake, pond, or large swimming pool. (Note: Always have an adult with you for safety when you are working around deep water.)

You need
- string
- 2 thermometers
- long pointed stick
- body of water
- a sunny day
- pencil and paper
- an adult

Tie string to each thermometer. At the end of a sunny day (about 5:00 p.m.), poke a hole 1 to 2 feet deep (30 to 60 cm) into the ground near a body of water with a long stick. A stake from a game of horseshoes or croquet works best. Lower one thermometer into the hole and tie the other end of the string to the stake. Then, hold the other thermometer in the water. Several minutes later, pull up both thermometers and read and record the temperatures. Take temperature readings every hour as the sun goes down and record your measurements on a chart. Compare the changes in temperature over time. Which lost heat faster, the land or the water? How do you think this affects the night temperatures of a town located at the edge of a large body of water? Were water and land both heated to the same temperature when you took the first reading?

Project 15
TESTING THE WATERS
An investigation of solar heat distribution

Does the water in a small lake evenly distribute the sun's heat energy, so that the temperature of surface water is the same as the water several feet down? Hypothesize, or guess, which you think will be warmer, the water on the surface of a small lake, the water several feet down, or the water at the edge, along the shoreline.

It is easy to take a lake's temperature near the shoreline. All you need to do is place a thermometer into the water at the edge of the lake. To read the real temperature of the lake's surface and some distance below is a little harder. The thermometers should be placed near the middle of the lake, or at least well out into it, not near the shore. This can be done without going out in a boat or into the water by constructing a small "boat" from wood, with one thermometer hanging below it and dragging a second, floating, thermometer off the back or stern of the boat.

First, find a standard size piece of wood about 6 inches long (15 cm) to serve as the boat that will tow the heat-measuring instruments. Tie a long piece of string to the regular thermometer and fasten the other end to the boat, using a thumbtack or nail. The thermometer should hang down at least 2 feet (60 cm) from the wooden boat. Tie a short piece of string to the thermometer that floats. Fasten the other end of the string to the boat also. Floating thermometers are often used in fish tanks and can be found at aquarium supply stores or pet shops.

You need
- thumbtacks or nails
- 6-inch-long (15 cm) piece of wood (1 by 2 or 2 by 4)
- fishing rod and reel
- string
- a thermometer
- a thermometer that floats (aquarium thermometer)
- metal washers
- a lake or pond
- pencil and paper
- an adult

Now that you are ready, ask an adult to take you and all your equipment to a nearby pond or lake and stand by to help with this experiment.

First, you need to find out the temperature of the lake at the shoreline. Bending carefully on the shore of the lake, place the thermometer in the water. Wait about three minutes to give the thermometer a chance to reach the proper temperature. Then remove the thermometer and immediately read and write down the temperature that it is registering.

To get the wooden boat out into the lake, lay it securely on the beach at the edge of the water or have your helper hold it there. Fasten the end of a fishing line from a fishing pole to the boat with a thumbtack. Slowly let out the line as you walk around the shore of the lake. (A helper could hold the boat and release it at your signal, when you get into position on the other side.) Carefully reel in the fishing line, dragging the boat and its "instruments" to a spot near the middle of the lake (or at least to a spot where the water is deep). Wait three or four minutes to allow the thermometers to properly change temperature. Then, reel the boat in as quickly as you can, and read the thermometers. The thermometers must be read before they begin to change temperature. The shoreline where you stand to reel in the boat should have sandy or a soft bottom, because quickly dragging the thermometers over a rocky bottom might break them.

Which thermometer read the warmest temperature? Was your hypothesis correct?

Project 16
OUR TOWN
Transforming and transporting energy

The light that comes from the lamp you read by in the evening is the result of energy changing forms several times and being transported over a great distance.

It all starts at a power plant. Energy from one of several sources is converted into electricity. Some plants burn fossil fuels (coal, oil, or natural gas), converting the solar energy stored in those fuels into heat. The heat is used to make steam that turns the shaft of generators (mechanical energy) to make electricity. Hydroelectric power plants use running water to turn the generators. Nuclear power plants harness radiation energy to make heat for steam generators.

You can show how energy can be changed from one form to another, transported over a distance, and then changed into another form of energy. The network of electric wiring in your community is a perfect example. Build a model town to demonstrate this process.

Use a 6-volt lantern battery to represent the electric power plant, where one form of energy is turned into another. (In the case of the battery, chemical energy inside it converts to electrical energy.) With hookup wire, connect three miniature (hobby) lamp sockets together.

Glue or tape flat sticks, or strong straws, together to form a cross or "T" shape These will serve as telephone

You need
- miniature 6-volt hobby lamps (bulbs)
- lamp sockets
- hookup wire
- jumper leads with alligator clip ends
- 6-volt lantern battery with spring-top connectors
- modeling clay
- flat sticks (from ice-cream bars) or strong straws
- glue or tape
- toy buildings used for model-train layouts
- wire cutters or scissors
- screwdriver

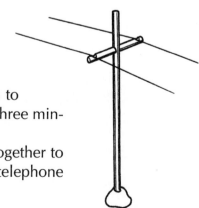

Schematic Diagram

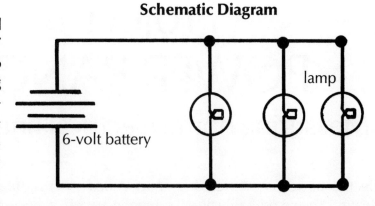

lamp

6-volt battery

poles. Make several of these "poles." Push each pole into a lump of modeling clay to hold it upright. Using the appropriate tool, cut a small notch in the top of each telephone pole arm. Place the hookup wire in the notches to hold them in place.

Using houses from a model-train or other set (or making your own out of cardboard), position them to form a small town. Put a lamp in each house to light it. The telephone poles should be positioned to run the wires from the battery and to the lamps in each home.

Energy is changed once again when it reaches each lamp. There, it is converted into light energy to illuminate the model homes, as it is in your own.

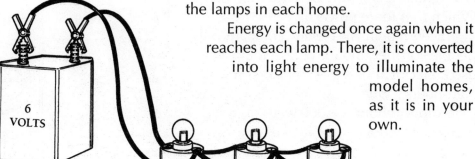

6 VOLTS

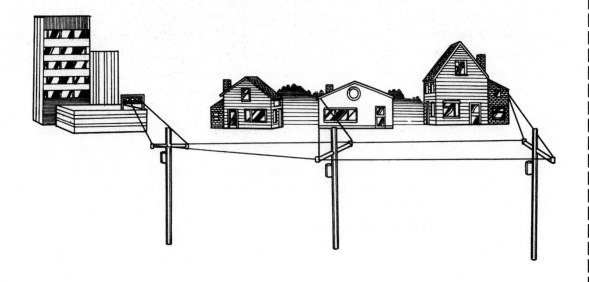

Project 17
POWER RANGER
Measuring home electrical energy usage

Electric power is measured in units called "watts." You've probably heard someone ask for a 40-, or 60-, or 100-watt bulb to change a burned-out light bulb. The number indicates how much electric power the bulb uses to reach full brightness. (Which do you think is brighter, a 60-watt or 100-watt bulb? Which uses more power?)

You need
- access to your home's electric meter
- pencil and paper

Every month, the electric company bills people for the amount of electricity they used. Electrical usage is measured in "kilowatt-hours." One kilowatt equals 1,000 watts. One kilowatt-hour is 1,000 watts of electric power being used for one hour. It takes one kilowatt-hour of energy to operate ten 100-watt light bulbs for one hour.

How much electrical energy does your home use in one day? Find the electric meter for your home (usually outside, where someone from the power company can find and read it easily). The meter's face has dials on it, marked with numbers. The dials, reading from right to left, show the ones, tens, hundreds, and then the thousands places. When a dial needle is between two numbers, it is the lower number that is read (a needle between 2 and 3 is read as 2).

Before school, read the numbers on the electric meter dials and write them down. The next day, at the same time, read the numbers again and record them. Subtract the second day's numbers from the first reading to find out how many kilowatt-hours of energy your home used over that 24-hour period.

Make a list of the appliances in your home that use electricity from the power company. Saving energy is good for the environment and will save your family money on the monthly electric bill too. How do you think you can use the appliances on your list more wisely to save energy in your home?

Project 18
FOOD ENERGY
The fuel of living things

For the human body to function, it needs energy. The energy for our bodies comes from the food we eat. Energy from foods is measured in units called calories. Our body changes the calories in the food we eat into energy to grow, maintain itself (stay well), and allow us to use our muscles to do work. In cold weather, the body needs more calories to do its work and keep us warm.

You need
- food labels, books, other research materials
- paper and pencil

A person who isn't going to drive very far doesn't need much gas in the car. But for a long trip, a car needs plenty of fuel. In the same way, a person who works at a desk and is not very active will not need as many calories as someone who mixes concrete and carries heavy cement blocks around all day. Some people cut down on the number of calories they eat in order to lose weight. When more calories are taken in than the body needs, it stores the rest as fat, causing the body to gain weight. Fat in the body is stored energy, but too much is not a good thing.

How many calories do you normally consume a day? For one day, list all the foods you eat—don't forget those between-meal snacks!—and how much. Look up how many calories there are in each food and make up a chart. Boxes of cereal and other foods list the amount of calories per serving—notice the number of servings per box. Books list the calories in different foods, such as: a ¼ pound hamburger patty, 224 calories; an orange, 50; ½ cup green beans, 15; an 8 ounce glass of milk, 150; a 6 ounce serving of ice cream, 290; one small chocolate chip cookie, 50. Total up the number of calories you ate during that one day.

Research how many calories a day are healthy for a person of your age and weight. Are you getting too many calories? Are you not eating enough to maintain a healthy body? How could you change your eating habits to cut down or raise the number of calories in your diet and still enjoy what you like?

Project 19
WHEN TO SAY WHEN
Measuring the energy (calorie) value of foods

You need
• research materials

Our bodies convert the food we eat into energy (see Project 18). Food energy is measured in calories. We need a certain amount of calories as fuel for our bodies, but taking in more calories than we need causes a person to gain weight.

Compare the number of calories in plain foods to the same type of foods that have sugar or something else added to them or are served in a different form. For example, compare the number of calories in a serving of popcorn to a serving of buttered popcorn. Compare the number of calories in a potato to a serving of french fries (or potato chips). Compare the calories in different candy bars that have the same weight. Compare the calories in a serving of peanuts to a serving of honey-roasted peanuts; a serving of whole milk with a serving of chocolate milk. Which foods have more calories?

What ingredients added in the cooking or processing of the foods increase the number of calories in them? By how much—a little, a lot? According to a published health chart, listing calorie needs for your age and weight, are there some foods you should avoid, or limit your intake of?

Project 20
SWEET SEARCH
An examination of sugar, the high-energy food

Foods sweetened with sugar do taste good! Unfortunately, too much sugar hurts our body's ability to use certain vitamins. It makes people gain weight, and causes tooth decay. Some children become hyperactive—that is, they can't sit still—when they take in too much sugar. Sugar comes in many different forms: sucrose, glucose (dextrose), fructose (found in fruits), lactose (found in milk), and maltose.

You need
- a trip to the super-market
- pencil and paper

Look at the labels on cereal boxes and compare the amount of calories per serving of cereals that are sugar-coated to those that are not. Usually, the ingredient that is contained in the cereal in the biggest proportion is listed first. Is the number-one ingredient usually sugar, or some form of sugar, in those cereals that are sugar-coated? Which cereals, sugar-coated or non-sugar-coated, do you think are better for your body?

Make a comparison chart showing the cereal's name, the number of calories per serving, and the amount of sugar per serving. Then make a chart comparing calories and sugar per serving of other foods that come in boxes and cans.

Not all labels will list the word "sugar" in the ingredients, even if there is sugar in it, be- cause, as we said, sugar comes in different forms. Research the different kinds of sugar found in our foods. For example, "high fructose corn syrup," a type of sugar, may be one ingredient listed on the label of a can or pork and beans.

Project 21
THE RIGHT STUFF
Seeds store enough food energy for germination

If you were traveling on foot for a long period of time, you would carry a backpack. In the back- pack you would store all the food you need to get you to the next camp, where you could replenish your food supply.

In the same way, seeds store just enough energy to be able to grow a root and a leaf. Once a seed has formed a root to gather water and nutrients from the soil and a leaf to collect sunlight, it can begin to make food on its own. The process of a plant making its food by gathering the light energy from the sun is called photosynthesis. Also needed in the process are carbon dioxide, water, chlorophyll (which gives leaves their green color), and very small amounts of minerals. The time from when a seed begins to sprout a root and a leaf (using its own stored energy) until it is able to make food on its own is called germination.

At your local hardware store or garden center, buy 3 different packages of seeds and a small bag of potting soil. The seeds can be flower or vegetable seeds.

Now, prove that seeds store enough energy to germinate, but then need sunlight to make food in order to continue to grow and live.

> **You need**
> - 3 different types of seeds (vegetable or flower)
> - potting soil
> - a dark place (a closet or basement)
> - water
> - 3 small containers (plastic drinking cups, etc.)
> - masking tape
> - pencil and paper

Fill 3 small containers with potting soil. Plastic drinking cups or short drinking glasses work well. Get 3 different kinds of seeds; they can be flower seeds (morning glory, marigold, etc.) or vegetable seeds (radish, lima bean, watercress, etc.). Place a piece of masking tape on the side of each container and on each write the name of the seeds you are going to plant in the container. Then put 5 of each kind of seed in their proper container (5 seeds are planted in case some do not germinate). Push the seeds about fi inch (about 13 cm) down into the soil.

Place the containers in a dark place (a closet, for example) that is at least as warm as room temperature all the time. Water the seeds every day. Keep the soil moist, but not heavily soaked.

Keep a written log of your observations each day. Write down the date and what you see in each container.

Once leaves appear, the stored food energy in the seeds is just about gone, and the plants are ready to begin making their own food. If the plants are kept in the dark and don't get any light to make new food, how long does it take for them to use up their stored energy and begin to die?

If you keep close watch and provide water and light at the right time, the young plants that start withering for lack of food may begin to start getting food from the soil. If not, plant new seeds and give them TLC (tender, loving care), and you may get to see them thrive.

Project 22
IN THE PINK
Home insulation keeps heat in and cold out

When the cold winter winds blow, we need to keep the heat energy from our home's heater inside. Builders use a material called "insulation" to keep warm air inside in the winter and cool, air-conditioned air inside in the summer. Insulation looks like thick blankets of cotton candy, usually pink or yellow in color. It is placed inside walls, ceilings, and sometimes under the floor.

Home insulation is given an "R-rating," which stands for how good a job that particular kind of insulation does. The higher the R-rating number, the better the insulation is at keeping the temperature on one side of the insulation from changing the temperature on the other.

How do we know that insulating materials do what they are supposed to? Let's prove it.

Remove the lid from a shoe box, or tear the flaps off of another box about the size of a shoe box. Stand the box upright on one end, so it is tall. With scissors, carefully cut a window in the "front" of the box,

You need
- 2 shoe boxes
- adhesive tape
- clear plastic food wrap
- scissors
- 2 thermometers
- modeling clay
- a sunny window
- sheets of Styrofoam about $\frac{1}{2}$ inch (1 cm) thick
- paper and pencil

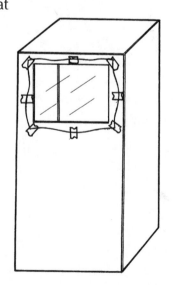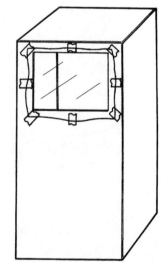

as shown. The window should be in the up-per ⅓ of the box. Then cover the window by taping a piece of clear plastic food wrap over it. Do the same to a second shoe box.

Turn the boxes around to work on the open "back" side.

Styrofoam is a light, usually white ma-terial. It is used for many things, including disposable coffee cups and for packing, so that appliances such as TV sets and micro-wave ovens are not damaged in shipping). It is also an insulating material, inexpensive, which is available in many shapes and sizes at hobby shops and craft stores.

Using adhesive tape or glue, line the bottom half of one shoe box with sections of Styrofoam, covering the three walls and making a "roof."

Inside each shoe box, place a small mound of modeling clay on the bot-tom. Turn a thermometer upside down and stick it in the clay. Do the same in the other box. The thermometers' bulbs will measure the air temperature in-side the boxes.

Cover the open backs of each box with a piece of clear plastic food wrap. Use adhesive tape to make the wrap fit tight.

Place both boxes in a sunny window, with the open "back" side of the boxes facing away from the sunlight. Be sure that the sunlight is not shining directly on the thermom-eter through the window in the uninsulated box.

Over a period of one or two hours, take readings and write down the tem-perature showing on both thermometers every five minutes. Does the air inside the insulated part of the shoe box stay cooler longer than the air in the uninsulated box?

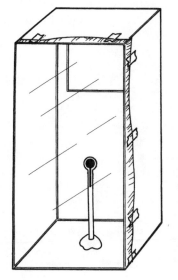
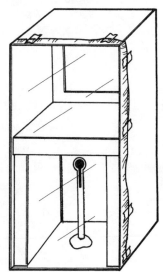

Project 23
KEEPING WARM
Insulating our bodies in cold weather

In the winter, your body needs more energy to keep you warm. We depend on our clothing to insulate us and keep us from losing our bodily warmth to the cold air when we are outside in bitter weather. What type of clothing material makes a good insulator?

Ask an adult to help you gather materials or fabrics to test as insulation. Find as many different kinds as you can. Look through old and worn clothing, that are not much use to anyone (ready to be thrown out, not "handed down" or donated). There might already be a bag of rags or scraps stored in a closet. Look over each item for a tag or label that tells what kind of material it is made of. Select several different kinds to test.

From each different piece of material, cut a square piece of it large enough to completely wrap around the top, bottom, and sides of a small jar (each piece of material should be the same size).

You need
- small jar
- several different kinds of material (an old T-shirt, towel, jeans, socks, linen, blanket, sweater)
- clock or watch
- warm tap water
- thermometer
- rubber bands
- scissors
- paper and pencil
- an adult

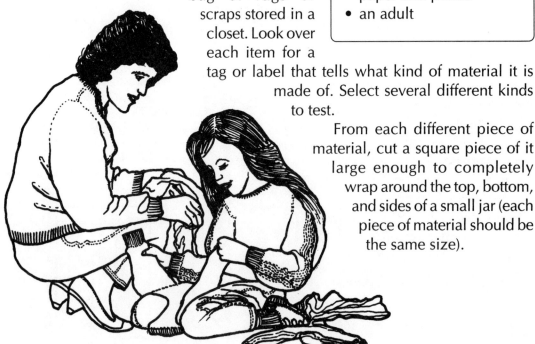

Turn the hot and cold water faucets on in your kitchen sink, and hold a thermometer in the stream. Adjust the faucets until the water is about body temperature (98.6 Fahrenheit/37 Celsius). Fill the jar with this water.

Quickly, stand the thermometer in the jar of water and wrap the jar completely with a piece of material, covering all the sides, bottom, and top. Use rubber bands to hold the material and the thermometer in place—the thermometer sticking up out of the jar.

Every five minutes, read the temperature on the thermometer (pull it up slightly if necessary and then slide it back down. Write the temperature down. Continue to record the temperature until it reaches the temperature of the room.

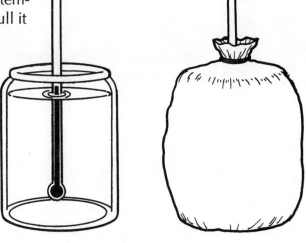

Fill the jar again with body-temperature water, and cover it with a different piece of material. Observe and record the temperature every five minutes until it reaches room temperature. Repeat this procedure for each piece of material you are testing.

(If you have someone to help you, and have more thermometers and same-size jars available, you could test the insulation of several kinds of material simultaneously, at the same time. Just be sure to keep your records straight when you read the temperatures.)

Which piece of material kept the water warm the longest? Do you know what it is made of? Polyester, rayon, cotton, etc.? Can you find out? Which material do you think would be best for making winter clothes? Which would be the worst?

Project 24
SHOCK TREATMENT
Capacitors and the storage of electrical energy

In the field of electronics, capacitors are components that perform many different tasks in an electronic circuit. One thing they do is temporarily store electricity. Unlike a battery, a capacitor must first be "charged up" with electricity.

Using modeling clay, make a base to hold two 1.5-volt "D" flashlight batteries together. The batteries should be laid down with the positive (+) end of one touching the negative (–) end of the other, just as they would be in a flashlight. The batteries are said to be "in series" with one another. When connected in this way, the total voltage across the two batteries is the sum of each battery: 1.5 volts + 1.5 volts = 3.0 volts.

You need
- 470-microfarad, 350-volt capacitor
- 2-volt T1-size light-emitting diode (LED)
- 2 "D" cell batteries (1.5-volt flashlight batteries)
- 2 insulated jumper leads with alligator clips on both ends
- modeling clay

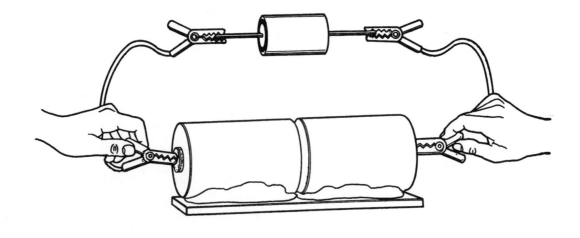

Connect one end of an insulated jumper lead to one of the leads (wires) coming from a 470-microfarad capacitor. Connect one end of another insulated jumper lead to the other lead coming from the capacitor. Note that batteries have a positive (+) and negative (–) marking on them. Also note that the capacitor also has positive and negative markings.

Taking the unconnected ends of the insulated jumper leads, hold the clip connected to the positive terminal on the capacitor to the positive terminal on the battery. Touch the clip connected to the negative terminal on the capacitor to the negative terminal on the battery for about 15 seconds. The capacitor should be charged.

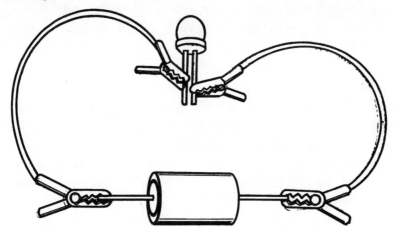

Now touch the leads from the capacitor to the leads of an LED, a light-emitting diode. While the LED does not have + and – markings, it does have + and – leads, and you must match the + of the capacitor to the + on the LED (and the – lead to the –). You will notice that one side of the LED is a little flatter than the other. The lead that comes from this side is the negative terminal (–).

When you touch the capacitor's leads to the LED, the LED will light brightly for about one second. Then, as it quickly uses up the electrical energy stored in the capacitor, you will see the light very quickly grow dimmer.

The ability of a capacitor to store an electrical charge is measured in microfarads, abbreviated UF. Would the LED glow brightly for a longer time if you used a capacitor that was rated at more than 470 microfarads?

Project 25
MARBLE ROLL
Converting kinetic energy into potential energy

Energy can be transferred from one object to another. "Kinetic energy" is the energy of an object in motion. If an object is moving and it hits another object, its energy is transferred, or handed over to the other object. On a pool table, players hit a ball with a cue stick, giving kinetic (movement) energy to the ball. When the ball rolls into another ball, all or part of this energy is given to the second ball, and the second ball begins to roll. Even though the first ball may stop, the force of kinetic energy continues on in the second ball.

> **You need**
> • marbles
> • 2 rulers
> • 2 books
> • a rug, or carpeted floor
> • piece of paper

Near a rug, or on a floor that has carpeting on it, lay two rulers next to each other, leaving a small space between them. Lay marbles back to back all along the space between the two rulers. Be sure the rulers are close enough together so that the marbles are not touching the floor—but are being held up by the rulers.

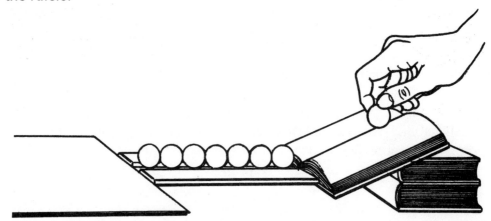

At one end of the rulers, open a book to about the middle. Make a ramp out of the open book by propping up the end opposite the rulers with another book.

Hold a marble at the top of the ramp. Let go. The force of gravity will give the marble motion energy. When the marble hits the first marble on the rulers, it hands its energy over to that marble. Being up against another marble and unable to move, that marble transfers its energy to the next marble. The energy continues to move from one marble to the next until the last marble is reached. When the energy is given to the last marble, it begins to roll, because there isn't anything blocking it. Is there enough energy to knock the last marble off the rulers? How far does it roll? The rug or carpet offers friction to the marble, and helps slow it down. Mark the spot where the marble comes to rest, or stops, with a tiny piece of paper.

Now, remove a few of the marbles so there are gaps between some of the marbles as shown in the illustration below. Roll the marble down the ramp again. Does the end marble roll as far? If not, why not? Do you think it may be because some of the energy was lost before getting to the last marble?

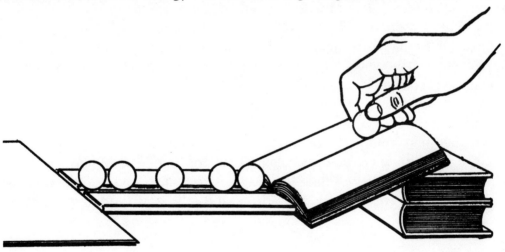

Project 26
FROLICKING IN THE WAVE
How some energies move

Energy can travel in the form of a wave. You are familiar with rolling waves in the ocean. Other types of energy waves, such as sound waves and radio waves, would look similar to ocean waves, if we could see them.

A wave has a "crest" or peak, the highest part of the wave, and it has a "trough" or valley, the lowest part. The length from crest to crest (or trough to trough) is called the "wavelength." The wavelength of a tsunami (a tidal wave) can be 100 miles (161 km) long! The wavelength of a 550 Hertz (cycles per second) sound wave, which is a note that is a little higher than "middle C" on a piano, is 2 feet (60 cm).

You need
- stiff paper
- thread
- pencils
- modeling clay
- string
- scissors
- quart milk cartons
- adhesive tape
- body of shallow water
- an adult

The same thing is true of waves in a lake or an ocean. When you see a rolling wave, it might look like the water is rolling, but very little water is actually moving. The water is only rising and falling as the force of energy

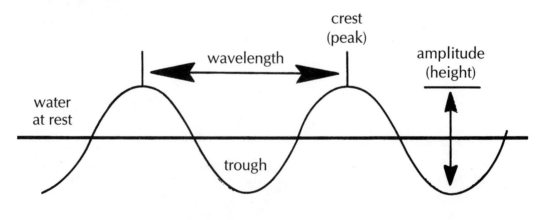

passes through it. A boat on the water will bob up and down as the wave energy moves under it. You can demonstrate this by placing a cork or a toothpick in a tub of water and dropping in a stone. The waves created by the stone entering the water will ripple out, and will push the cork or toothpick up and down.

Have a friend hold lightly on to one end of a long jump rope As you hold the other end, quickly whip your end up and down. You will see the rope take the shape of a wave, and travel down the rope toward the other end. If your friend is holding the rope, when the energy gets to his end, it will yank the rope out of his hand.

Now tie one end of the jump rope to a fence. Quickly whip your end up and down, again and again, and set up a wave pattern. If you want to measure the "amplitude" or height of the wave, have a friend stand along side the rope and hold up a measuring stick, and watch where the lowest point (the trough) and the highest point (the crest) fall.

Fill a round cake pan half full of water. Fill an eye dropper with water. You can find the exact center of the pan by squeezing a drop of water into the pan and causing rippling waves. If you squeeze a drop of water perfectly in the center, the waves will ripple out to the edges of the pan, then back again, and meet exactly at the center point. If the waves didn't meet back together, wait until the water calms; then keep trying it until you find the exact center.

Sound wave energy can also travel through other materials besides air. Put your ear on the metal pipe of a chain link fence and have a friend tap a nail on the pipe at the other end. You will hear the sound travel through the pipe.

Project 27
LITTLE SIR ECHO
Making use of sound waves to measure distance

The energy of a sound wave travels through the air at about 1100 feet, or 335 meters, per second. In projects 24 and 25, we saw how energy waves travel through a medium (air, water, metal, etc.) but that the molecules of the medium don't actually travel forward with the wave.

> **You need**
> • a large building
> • tape measure
> • friends

As a rolling wave moves through the ocean, the wave energy moves forward, but the actual molecules of water only move up and down with the wave's crest and trough. That is why a boat on the water will bob up and down, but not move forward, as a rolling wave goes by. This concept can also be shown by tying a piece of ribbon onto the middle of a jump rope, then tying one end of the rope to a fence, and moving the other end up and down, setting up waves. The ribbon will go up and down, but not forward in the direction of the wave.

The energy of sound waves also travels in the same way. Molecules in the air bump into each other and push the wave along, but the actual molecules travel very little.

Since we know that sound travels at about 1100 feet per second, we can use it to determine distance. You are probably familiar with counting "one one thousand, two one thousand, three one thousand," to count the seconds between seeing a flash of lightning and hearing the rumble of thunder. Since 1100 feet is about one-fifth of a mile, a gap of one second between seeing a lightning flash and hearing its thunder indicates that the lighting was about one-fifth of a mile away.

Have you ever gone into an empty room and heard your voice echo off the walls? When your ears hear two sounds that are about one-tenth second or longer apart, your brain interprets those as two distinct sounds...an echo, if the two sounds are the same (a loud yell, for example). Traveling at 1100 feet per second, it takes a sound wave about one-tenth of a second to go 110 feet. If you yell at a large wall, you will hear an echo if the sound travels 110 feet or more to get back to you. That would mean you are 55 feet from the wall, because the sound would have to travel to the wall and back to you (55 x 2 = 110).

Find a building that has a broad wall, perhaps your school building. Face the wall and stand about 30 feet away from it. Yell loudly at the wall. Take a step backward and yell again. Continue to move back until you hear your voice echo. Then, using a tape measure, measure the distance from the wall to where you stood when you first heard an echo. Is the distance about 55 feet?

Have your friends try it. Record the distance where each friend first hears his echo. Are the distances close to 55 feet? Add the distances together and divide by the number of friends to find the average distance. How close is the average distance to 55 feet?

Project 28
ENERGY UNLEASHED
The hazards of fast-moving water

Many people have built homes on the beach by the ocean. It's a beautiful place to live...until a hurricane comes!

The kinetic energy of moving water can be very powerful. Water moving normally in a river or stream bed usually stays where it should. But large volumes of fast-moving water can overflow the riverbanks, gouging out huge troughs and, like a bulldozer, pushing over cars, houses, and anything in its path.

Set this project up outdoors. Cover an area about 2 by 3 feet (60 by 90 cm) with sand, piling it to a height of about an inch. Make a riverbed in the sand by scooping out a 2 to 3 inch wide (5 by 7.5 cm) channel from one end to the other of the 3-foot (90 cm) length.

Place some small-scale model buildings along the edge of the "river." Buildings from an HO train set or other small-scale models work well, or you can make your own buildings using cardboard and adhesive tape. Also, place some buildings away from the riverbed, making a town.

Cut a 2 by 4 foot (60 by 120 cm) piece of corrugated cardboard from a box (have an adult help you). Fold the piece of cardboard in half, lengthwise—along the 4-foot (120 cm) length. Then open it up again, but not all the way, making a "V" shape. To keep the top of the cardboard from getting wet, cover it with plastic food wrap or aluminum foil. Use tape to hold it in place. The cardboard "V" will be a slope or ramp that will channel water into the riverbed when water is poured into it.

You need
- sand
- 4 two-liter plastic soda bottles
- water
- small houses and buildings (scale train-set models,for example)
- large dishpan
- several thick books
- piece of corrugated or stiff cardboard, about 2 by 4 feet (60 by 120 cm)
- plastic food wrap
- adhesive tape
- an area outside

At one end of the riverbed, place the end of the cardboard ramp. Raise the other end of the ramp to a height of about 6 inches (15 cm) by placing several thick books or blocks of wood under it. To keep it in a "V" shape to make a water chute, stack books on both sides.

Fill four 2-liter plastic soda bottles with water. Very slowly pour water out of each bottle onto the high end of the ramp, allowing the water to trickle through the riverbed in the model town. After the bottles are empty, look at the river bed and all the buildings in the town. Write down any changes that you see.

Fill the four bottles with water again. Now empty all of the bottles into a large dishpan. Dump all of the water quickly, at once, down the ramp. The same amount of water now travels through the river as before, but the first release consisted of slow-moving water over a long period of time, and during the second release it is fast-moving water over a very short period of time. Now, when this "flash flood" or hurricane surge of water hits the town, what happens to the riverbed? What happens to the buildings along the river? What happens to the buildings that were not next to the river?

Note: If you have access to a still camera, take "before," "during," and "after" pictures. A camcorder (videotape recorder and camera system) can even capture the live action as it happens.

Do more research into hurricanes, floods, and erosion.

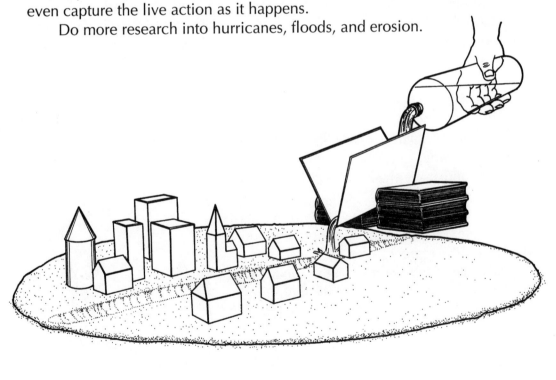

Project 29
SUN, YOU'RE TOO MUCH!
Taming solar energy the natural way

Heat energy from the sun is usually thought of in a good way because of the many benefits. But there are times when this heat is unwanted. Have you ever walked on a beach when the sun made the sand so hot that you had to run or put shoes on your feet? Or gotten into a car "baking" in the hot summer sun with the windows closed up?

You need
- thermometer
- a sunny day
- a large shady tree
- pencil and paper

In winter, bright warm sunshine streaming through the windows of your home helps keep you comfortable inside. But in summer, this *extra* heat causes fans and air conditioners to work even harder, as they try to cool the house.

Trees can provide natural shading for homes. By planting trees along the side of a house where the hot summer sun beats, a home can be kept cooler naturally, and save electrical energy.

Let's prove that trees lower the temperature of the air in their shade. On a hot sunny day, find a large tree and stand in its shade. There, hold a thermometer out at shoulder height, being careful not to touch the bulb. Wait several minutes for the temperature to settle, then read the thermometer and write down the temperature.

Now, stand in the open, in the sun away from any shade. Again, hold out the thermometer and wait for the temperature to settle. Then read and write down the temperature.

Which location had the lower temperature?

Project 30
THE GREEN SCREEN
Trees as natural wind-energy protection

Protecting a home from strong, cold winter winds would certainly help to keep heat energy inside the house and lower energy costs.

> **You need**
> • art and construction supplies

Farms often have large open areas in which acres of crops are planted. To slow strong winds down and protect their crops and topsoil from wind damage, and their homes from cold, farmers often plant trees in a row to grow tall and cut the prevailing winds. Long ago, during long, cold winters, such windbreaks were especially important to the families living in farmhouses, when insulating materials and efficient means of heating weren't as good as today.

Using art and construction supplies or scale models (the kind used for train sets), construct a model of a farm, showing its open crop-filled fields, the farmhouse, and where rows of trees would be placed to act as windbreaks. Research weather maps in the area of your "farm" for wind direction.

Again, using art and construction supplies or models, construct a model of a home or apartment dwelling in a city. A city home may only have exposure to the wind in the front and back, if it is attached or very close to other buildings on both its sides. Other people's homes or apartments will act as windbreaks for the person's home in the middle.

Project 31
CHOOSE NOT TO LOSE

Identifying causes of home heat-energy loss

The wood in your home or apartment's walls and roof, along with insulation material, does a good job of keeping heat inside in the winter and cool air inside in the summer. Wood is a natural in-sulator. It has millions of tiny cells, sort of like a honeycomb. These cells

You need
• your home
• a windy day
• pencil and paper

are natural pockets that trap air, and air does not conduct heat. Home-building experts say that about 75 percent of a door's heat loss occurs around its edges. That is why people sometimes stuff newspaper or old rags around the edges of an unused door, and push a throw rug against its bottom. Heat energy can also be lost around windows, and electrical outlets and switches.

Investigate your house for places where drafts can enter and rob your house of heat energy. Draw a floor plan of your house, showing where windows, doors, electrical outlets, and electrical switches are located. Then go to each location and check for the presence of a draft. Pay attention to the sensitive soft cheeks of your face; they are a great way to feel moving air. On your floor plan, write down any locations where you feel a draft.

You might see evidence of a draft by holding something light, such as a very small down feather or tiny piece of lint from a clothes dryer's trap, up to where you suspect air leakage.

Have your parents or an adult take you to the local hardware or building-supply store and research ways that would help keep heat from leaking out of these drafty locations.

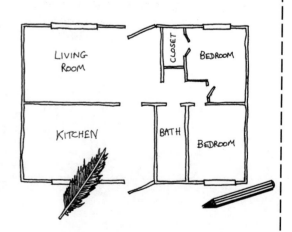

Project 32
NOW YOU HEAR IT...
Tracking radio frequency direction

At radio and television stations, powerful transmitters send radio waves out of the antenna and through the air, on their way to your radio receiver or TV set. Can you use a radio as a direction finder in order to locate the station that a radio wave is coming from?

You need
- inexpensive AM pocket radio
- aluminum foil
- table

Take an inexpensive AM pocket radio and place it on the table. Tune it to a station that is coming in strongly and clearly. Fold a piece of aluminum foil in a shape of a cave or pocket and place it around the top, bottom, and three sides of the radio, leaving only the front of the radio showing in the opening. Place the radio back in position on the table.

Is the station still coming in as strong? Slowly turn your radio, along with its aluminum shield, exposing the open front side to different directions. Is the station still coming in as strong? Continue to turn it around until you have made a complete circle. If the station is strongest when facing one particular direction, then that is the direction that radio waves are coming from.

Do the experiment with several other radio stations. Are the signals coming from the same or different directions? List the stations, by their ID letters or where they are on the radio dial, and write down the direction of their signal transmitter.

Project 33
ONCE, TWICE, AGAIN
Reusing products to save energy

It takes energy for a factory to make a product. If that product can be used twice, or used to do more than one job, that reduces the need to make more of the product—saving energy.

What items around your home or school can be used more than once, or used in a different way after their first use? Plastic products are often handy to keep for other uses. Responses to a recent consumer poll suggest that 87 percent of Americans had reused a plastic product over the previous six-month period.

You need
- various materials from around the house (plastic soda bottles, paper grocery bags, plastic bags, plastic margarine tubs, etc.)
- pencil and paper

SOME ADDED USES FOR MANUFACTURED PRODUCTS

Plastic soda bottles
1. Make into bird feeders.
2. To store cold drinking water in refrigerator.
3. Use as a terrarium.
4. Experiments.
5. A penny bank.
6. Pocket money—return bottles to store for refund.

Can you think of other uses for bottles, and for the other products

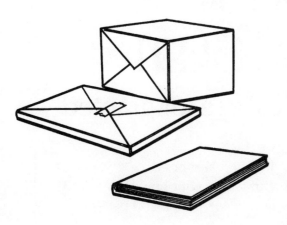

Paper grocery bags
1. Bring to grocery, when out shopping, to pack order.
2. As covers for school textbooks.
3. To carry things, such as gifts, when visiting relatives.
4. To wrap packages for mailing.
5. For arts and crafts projects, such as masks for plays or Halloween.
6. Spread out to protect work area.
7. Place them in your community's recycling trash pickup.

Plastic margarine tubs
1. To store screws or small items.
2. To store food leftovers.
3. As scoop—for dog food, animal feed, fertilizer.
4. To catch water under small flower pots.
5. With puncture holes in bottom to sprinkle water on plants.
6. As beach toys, to hold sand and water, or use as molds for sand castles.

Plastic grocery bags
1. Line small bedroom wastebaskets.
2. To carry school lunches that may be soggy or might leak.
3. To put carried books or packages in when it starts to rain.
4. When packing a wet bathing suit.
5. To hold wet laundry to hang or dry.
6. To keep feet, or shoes, dry in rainstorm.
7. To collect recyclables for pickup.

Tip: Stuff each bag, one by one, into the top of an old stocking and cut a hole in the toe to make a handy plastic bag dispenser!

Project 34
UNPLUGGED!

Taking home electrical use for granted

The development of electrical energy has been a wonderful benefit to mankind. But society has become very dependent on electricity. Sometimes the power coming into our homes is interrupted. We take the many things

You need
- your home
- pencil and paper

that work by electrical power for granted—until the power is lost! This can happen when there is trouble with the electric utility equipment, lightning strikes a telephone pole, strong storm winds blow down power lines, or too many people simply use too much electricity all at once or for too long.

Losing electric power to a home means that many things we normally do, without giving them much thought, suddenly become inconvenient. Some are only small inconveniences, such as using candles or flashlights instead of electric lights for a few hours. You may not be able to watch your big-screen TV, but you can still read, play a game, or listen to a battery-operated radio.

However, the loss of electrical power can cause serious problems. If the power fails during the winter and your home is warmed by electric heat, a loss of electricity could make the house uncomfortably cold. If your home has its own water well, an electric water pump cannot work without power. The kitchen sink is not normally thought of as being electrical, but if the water pump is out, you can't bring water into the pipes; so there is no water for drinking, cooking, washing, or for flushing a toilet. No water can be a very serious problem.

What things around your home would stop working if the electric power should go off? What things around your home use energy but are not connected to and dependent on the electric utility company? Examples would be a candle, a wind-up toy, a flashlight, a watch, and a kerosene lamp. Can any of these items be used to replace an item that uses electric power from the power company, and save electricity? A wind-up clock could replace an electric clock; it would require you to wind it up every day, but that would save electrical energy. However, a battery-operated radio would not efficiently replace a radio that runs on house current, because batteries are more expensive.

Project 35
TREASURE HUNT
Your neighborhood with/without electrical power

When Thomas Edison and his team of scientists perfected the electric light bulb long ago and began building electric stations to generate power, towns and cities took on a whole new look.

You need
- arts and crafts supplies
- your neighborhood or a nearby town

Walk down your street or around your neighborhood and imagine what it would look like without electrical energy. What would be missing? Would you see streetlights? Flashing traffic signals? How about those bright, neon signs in storefronts? Television antennas? People lined up at bank ATM machines? A fire box? Satellite dish? Telephone poles? Transmission towers?

Make two drawings, one showing what your street or neighborhood looks like and another of what the same scene would look like if electricity had not been developed.

Project 36
LOOKING UP
Most of Earth's energy comes from our sun

Almost all energy on the Earth comes from the sun's energy (geothermal, tidal, and nuclear are the only ones that do not).

Wind is caused by the uneven heating of the Earth's surface by the sun. Waves in a large body of water can be the result of winds. Wood, used for many things including firewood to heat homes, comes from trees, which require sunlight to grow. Oil products (coal, gas, oil, kerosene, and propane) are formed by rotting plants and wood, packed down tightly and under great pressure for many centuries.

The energy of moving water in streams is partly caused by the sun's energy. Rivers, streams, and waterfalls are the result of evaporation caused by the sun's energy. The water then falls back to Earth as rain, snow, or some other form of precipitation, and gravity moves it from a higher to a lower level.

Electrical energy for our homes is generated at a power plant often by burning a fossil fuel such as coal. Hydroelectric power is generated by water moving through great turbines. Construct a model showing objects that represent the types of energy on Earth that directly or indirectly are the result of solar energy.

Project 37
NUCLEAR DOMINOS
Demonstrating a chain reaction

One type of energy is released when the nuclei of atoms are either combined (fusion) or split apart (fission). The energy, called "nuclear energy," is released in the form of heat, light, or some other type of radiation. Nuclear energy is used to make electricity by heating water for steam that then drives giant turbine generators.

In the process of nuclear fission, the splitting apart of an atom causes a chain reaction. A radioactive element, such as Uranium-235, is used in the chain reaction. The first fission creates two new neutrons. Each of these neutrons strikes at least two other neutrons, which strike even more, and a chain reaction takes place which continues to grow.

To demonstrate the concept of nuclear fission, stand dominos in the pattern shown, where one domino is set to start a chain reaction. As it falls, the domino hits two dominos, which each hit two more. The number of dominos hit and falling with each row grows quickly. This chain reaction of falling dominos can be demonstrated easily using only 4 or 5 rows; with additional rows the arranged dominos become so packed together that they get in each other's way.

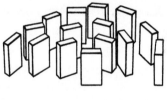

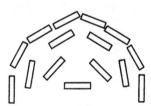

In a nuclear reactor where nuclear fission is taking place, the chain reaction can be slowed down or even stopped by inserting rods made of cadmium or boron. These dampening rods absorb neutrons and slow the process down. Demonstrate this by placing a ruler between two dominos in a row, then push the first domino to start the chain reaction. The reaction stops when it reaches the ruler, which acts like the rods in a nuclear reactor.

Project 38
ENERGY STOPPER
Friction and the reduction of energy

Friction is a force that can act on a moving object to slow it down, requiring the use of additional energy if it is to be kept going. Friction is caused by two objects rubbing together. When you are ice skating or riding a sled down a snowy hill, friction tries to reduce your rate of motion. The metal runners on skates and sleds are specially designed to reduce friction so that you are able to go faster.

To demonstrate friction and how it can rob energy, cover a piece of cardboard about 1 foot (30 cm) square with clear plastic food wrap. Pull the food wrap tightly across the cardboard and use adhesive tape underneath to keep it tight. Take the cardboard outside and lay it on a flat surface, such as a driveway or sidewalk.

Place a dry bar of soap in the middle of the board. Hold one end and slowly raise it, making a ramp, until the bar of soap begins to slide. At this point, the force of gravity is stronger than the friction. Place the zero-marked end of a ruler or measuring stick on the flat surface and hold its scale markings against the high end of the cardboard ramp. Write down how many inches or centimeters high it had to be to overcome friction.

> **You need**
> • clear plastic food wrap
> • adhesive tape
> • bar of soap
> • water
> • cardboard, about 1 foot (30 cm) square
> • ruler, yardstick, or meter stick
> • a flat surface outside (sidewalk, driveway, porch, etc.)
> • pencil and paper

Next, thoroughly wet the bar of soap and pour water onto the cardboard ramp. A watering can would work well for this job. Will water reduce the friction?

Place the bar of soap at the exact spot where it was before, at the middle of the ramp. Lift the end of the ramp until the bar of soap overcomes friction and begins to slide. Measure the height of the ramp. Did the ramp have to be raised as high, before the soap moved the second time?

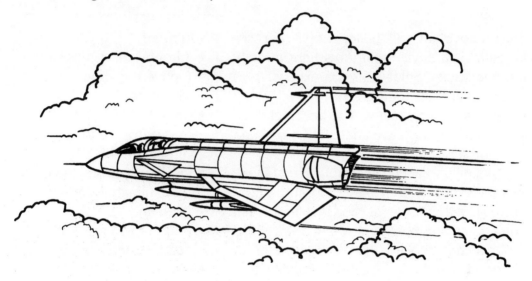

Moving through the air causes friction, too. It can increase the energy usage of cars, planes, and other vehicles—which is why they are designed to be as "aerodynamic" as possible. Do more research on how friction can be an energy robber.

Project 39
CELL MAGIC
Changing light energy to electrical energy

The photovoltaic cell, better known as a "solar cell," is a device that turns light directly into electricity. Solar cells are expensive to manufacture, so they are only used when there is no other easier way to get electricity, such as at a remote weather station or in an Earth-orbiting satellite.

A single solar cell does not generate very much electricity, but solar cells can be connected together "in series" and their individual voltages added together. Connecting cells in series means hooking the positive (+) terminal of one cell to the negative (–) terminal of the next. Flashlights have their batteries connected in series, with the negative terminal of one battery touching the positive terminal on the next. When batteries are connected in series, the total voltage available across all of them is the sum of the individual battery voltages as shown. Imagine how much more power you could exert on a rope if the strength of three of your friends were also helping you to pull it.

You need
- 3 hobby solar cells (delivering about $1/2$ volt each)
- small DC hobby motor (requiring $1^1/2$ to 3 volts direct current)
- insulated jumper leads with alligator clips on each end
- a sunny window with a shade, blinds, or curtain
- several small wooden blocks

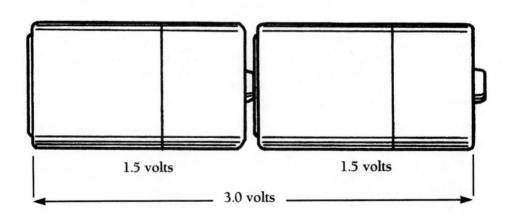

1.5 volts   1.5 volts

3.0 volts

Using insulated jumper leads with alligator clips on each end, connect the positive and negative terminals of a solar cell to a small 1.5-volt hobby motor. Set the arrangement in a sunny place. Use wood blocks behind the cells to tilt them so that they face the sun. You could also use spring-type clothespins clipped onto the sides near the bottoms of the cells to stand them upright. Watch how fast the motor spins. Next, add two more solar cells to the circuit, placing them in series.

Look at and listen to the motor. Is it spinning faster now that it is getting more voltage? What happens to the motor's speed on a cloudy day?

Create your own "cloudy day" by closing blinds or curtains partway, then all the way. Do you think the voltage produced by the solar cells is less on cloudy days? How do you think that affects the location of where solar cells work best?

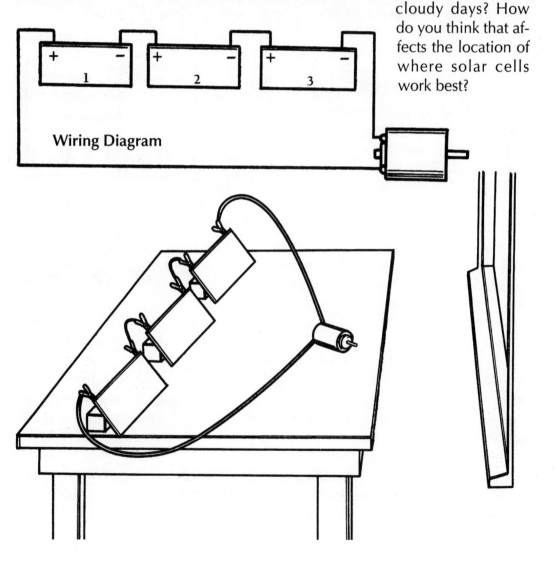

Wiring Diagram

Project 40
HEAT LOST?
Using energy to remove (transfer) heat

The invention of the refrigerator has been a tremendous benefit to people, keeping foods from spoiling quickly. When the refrigerator runs, what happens to the air inside it? Where does the heat go? It doesn't just disappear. The refrigerator actually moves it out into the room.

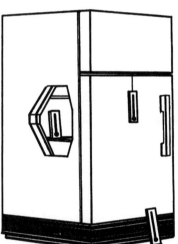

You need
- 3 thermometers
- refrigerator
- string

To cool the air inside a refrigerator, another energy source is needed—electricity. Tubes inside the refrigerator are filled with a fluid called "refrigerant." It absorbs heat. With the help of an electric motor, the heated fluid goes through a "condenser" and the fluid gives up its heat to the surrounding air. The condenser is made up of coils and is found either on the back of your refrigerator or at the bottom. If you don't see the coils behind it, look under the refrigerator.

Put a thermometer inside the refrigerator, and another one near the condenser coils, wherever they are on your refrigerator. Tie a piece of string to a third thermometer and hang it on the front door, near the middle, to measure the room temperature.

Wait for the refrigerator's condenser motor to turn on, which it will do occasionally when the temperature inside the refrigerator rises above the temperature that its thermostat is set at. Listen for the motor to stop in a few minutes. When it does, read the temperatures on all of the thermometers. Is the temperature near the condenser coils warmer than the room temperature shown on the thermometer hanging on the door?

Air conditioners use the same principle. If you have a window air conditioner running, try placing a thermometer inside it and one on its outside. Is the heat from the room being moved to the outdoors?

Project 41
BRIGHT HEAT
Unwanted heat energy from incandescent light

The most common types of home lighting are incandescent and fluorescent bulbs. In both, electrical energy is turned into light energy.

In an incandescent light bulb, electricity passes through a small wire, called a filament, which glows brightly. In a fluorescent light bulb (usually a long straight or circular tube), the inside of the bulb is filled with a gas. The inside glass of the bulb is coated with materials called phosphors. When electricity is passed through a heating element in the bulb, the gas gives off rays that cause the phosphors to fluoresce (glow).

> **You need**
> - light from a fluorescent tube
> - light from an incandescent bulb
> - thermometer
> - pencil and paper
> - an adult

All we really want from a light bulb is light. However, in the changing of electrical energy into light energy, there is energy loss. Some of that energy is given off as heat, especially unwelcome during hot weather! Which type of light bulb is more energy-efficient (gives off less heat to the surrounding air)?

Find a lamp in your home that uses an incandescent bulb (most lamps do). Find a fluorescent lamp (fluorescent bulbs are often used in kitchens, bathrooms, garages, and workshop areas). Remember, when working around hot light bulbs and electrical fixtures, to have an adult with you. A light bulb may stay quite hot even after it has been turned off, and it can cause a burn.

Remove the shade from a lamp that has an incandescent bulb. Hold the bulb of a thermometer about one inch (2.5 cm) away from the lit bulb for about three minutes. Record the temperature. Now do the exact same procedure using a lit fluorescent bulb. Record that temperature. Which bulb is more light-efficient?

Project 42
UNEQUAL ENERGY
Finding the distribution of heat energy in a room

Is the temperature in a room the same everywhere in the room? You might think that it is. But as you do this project, you may be surprised to discover that the air temperature is different in different parts of the room—the heat energy in the room is not equally distributed.

Pick about ten different locations in a large room in your home. Some locations should be high up, some low near the floor, some on an "inside" wall (a wall with another room behind it), and some on an "outside" wall (with the outdoors on the other side). High locations can be above an inside door (over the open doorway or,

You need
- a large room in your house
- thermometer
- a clock or watch
- paper and pencil
- an adult

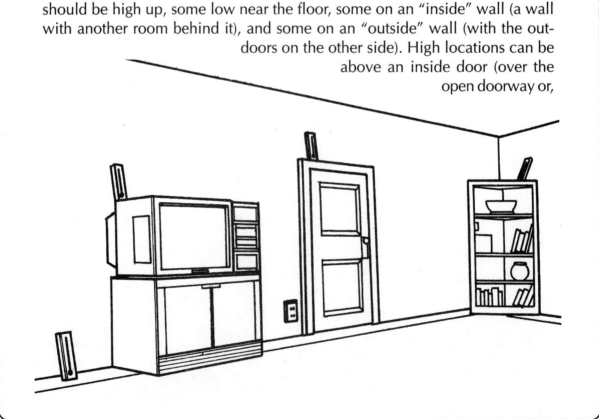

with the door ajar, the thermometer lying on top) or on top of a picture frame on a wall. Ask an adult to help you place thermometers in the highest places. One of the locations should be by a window, another by an electric light switch on an outside wall.

Make a chart with two columns and at the head of the first column write "locations"; then list the locations you've selected. At the top of the second column write "temperature."

Put the thermometer at your first location. Wait about three minutes to give the thermometer time to adjust and indicate the correct temperature. Write down the temperature reading for that location. Repeat this procedure for all of the locations in your room.

Compare the temperatures you have taken around the room. Which location is the warmest? Which is the coolest? Why do you think the temperature may be different at each location? Look up the word "convection" in the dictionary. Do you think poor insulation by a light switch on an outside wall or by a window might be affecting the air temperature at that location?

Project 43
BAND AT TENSION
Mastering potential energy in a stretched elastic band

When you pull the elastic band of a slingshot back as far as it will go and hold it, the elastic band has potential (stored) energy, ready to do work. When you let go, that potential energy is released to do work. This energy in motion is called kinetic energy.

How can we show that the more a rubber band is stretched, the more potential energy it has (and the more kinetic energy is released when you let go of the rubber band)?

Let's construct a paper towel tube "cannon" and use a Ping-Pong ball as a cannonball to measure kinetic energy when it is shot out of the cannon. Don't use anything heavier as the cannonball, because flying objects can be dangerous. A Ping-Pong ball is safe to use.

Take two pieces of masking tape about 4 inches (10 cm) long. Lay them on top of each other, with sticky sides touching..

Fold the masking tape over one end of an empty paper towel roll. Position it so that it covers only a part of the paper towel roll opening as shown. Use another piece of masking tape to hold it onto the roll. This tape will act as a "stopper" by making the opening just small enough to keep the ball from falling through, but will let it stick out of the bottom a little. Lay the roll aside for now.

You need
- Ping-Pong ball
- masking tape
- empty paper towel roll
- thick book
- measuring tape
- rubber band
- board, about 3 to 4 inches (8 to 10 cm) wide and 1 foot (30 cm) long
- ruler
- 2 nails
- hammer
- paper and pencil

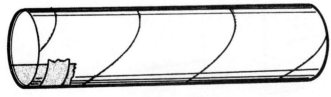

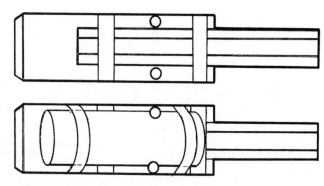

Using masking tape, tape a ruler to a piece of wood about 3 or 4 inches (8 to10 cm) wide by 1 foot (30 cm) long. Let about 5 to 6 inches (13 to15 cm) of the ruler hang over one end of the board.

Hammer two nails part of the way into the board, one on each side near the outside edges, about 3 inches (7.5 cm) from the end of the board where the ruler is. Leave the nails sticking up slightly.

Lay the paper towel roll on top of the ruler and board assembly, between the nails, and fix it in place with masking tape. Set your "cannon" on the floor.

Elevate the front end of the cannon by placing a book under the end opposite the ruler. Put a rubber band across the two nails, stretching it around the bottom of the paper towel tube. Drop your "cannonball" into the tube so it comes to rest at the bottom of the tube, on the masking-tape stopper and the rubber band.

Using the scale on the ruler, pull the rubber band back 1 inch (2.5 cm) and let go. The rubber band will hit the ball and shoot it out of the cannon. Watch where the ball first touches the floor. Use a tape measure to find the distance the ball traveled out of the cannon. Make a chart to record how far back the rubber band is pulled and how far the ball travels through the air.

Next, pull the rubber band back 1½ inches (4 cm). Measure and record the distance the ball travels. Repeat this procedure, ½ inch (1 cm) at a time, until the rubber band has been stretched back as far as it can.

Look at your chart of data. Does the ball travel farther if the rubber band is pulled farther back? Is there a mathematical relationship (a number pattern) between the distance the rubber band is pulled back and the distance the ball goes? For example, does the ball go 1 foot (30 cm) farther for each inch (2.5 cm) the rubber band is pulled back?

Project 44
LESS THAN BRIGHT
Brownouts in electric power service

The demand for electrical energy by those living in our cities and communities changes constantly. For example, on very hot summer days, more people use fans and air conditioners, so the demand on electricity from the power company is higher.

What happens if a 10-megawatt power plant tries to deliver $10\frac{1}{2}$ megawatts during a time of such high demand? A power company may choose to lower the voltage going out a little, so there is enough to go around to everyone. This is called a "brownout." A power plant representative told us that when demand for electricity goes higher than the plant can produce, the power company can reduce power by 5, 10, or even 15 percent. Most people won't even notice a 5 or 10 percent reduction in power.

In a really bad situation, when more electricity is needed than even a brownout can help with, the power plant may have to turn power off to different areas, each area losing power for 15 minutes at a time. This is called a "rolling blackout." By losing power for only 15 minutes, most people are only slightly inconvenienced.

When a brownout occurs, the normal voltage available to the electrical appliances in your home is reduced. In lamps during a brownout, light bulbs may not shine as brightly as normal.

Although running a light bulb at a lower voltage will not harm it, lower voltages for a long period of time can damage motors. To make up for the voltage drop, a motor will draw more current. The increased flow of electricity through the motor's "windings" (coils of wire inside) makes the wire heat up. This can destroy the motor. Motors can be found in many places around the house: refrigerators, water pumps, air conditioners, swimming pool pumps,

You need
- 3 "D" flashlight battereies (1.5 volts)
- insulated jumper leads with alligator clips on both ends
- modeling clay
- small board or piece of cardboard
- 2 flashlight bulbs (3 volts)

fans, and forced hot-air heaters all have motors. If a brownout occurs at your house, alert an adult to turn off appliances until the power returns to normal.

To get a taste of a brownout, in this project we will operate a flashlight bulb at only half the voltage it is designed to take and compare it to a bulb getting full voltage. Using modeling clay, make a base to hold two 1.5-volt "D" flashlight batteries together. The batteries should be laid on a small board or piece of cardboard, with the positive (+) end of one touching the negative (–) end of the other, just as they would be in a flashlight. The batteries are said to be "in series" with one another. When connected in this way, the total voltage across the two batteries is the sum of each battery: 1.5 volts + 1.5 volts = 3.0 volts.

Clip one end of an insulated jumper lead to the small metal tip of a flashlight bulb. Clip one end of another insulated jumper lead to the wide metal base of the bulb. Touch the other two ends of the jumper leads to the batteries as shown.

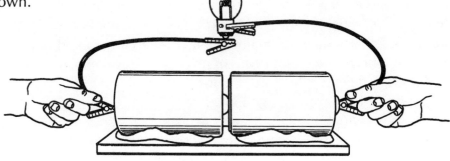

Make another identical setup, but this time only use one battery. Compare the brightness of the two bulbs.

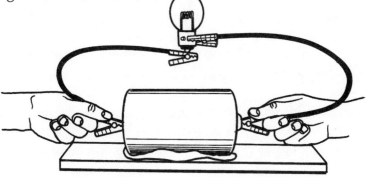

Call your local electric power company and research more information about brownouts and blackouts.

Project 45
ENERGY DETECTIVE
Helping your school save energy

When energy is used inefficiently by your school, it not only wastes valuable resources, it also costs your family, neighbors, and community money by increasing the school's expenses. Is your school conserving energy? Do an investigative study and give your school a report on its use of energy.

Start your investigation by talking to one of your school's custodians or maintenance people. Ask about the insulation in the school's walls and ceiling, how old the insulation is, if it is missing or damaged in some areas, if there is enough insulation. Ask the custodian about the heat and light in classrooms after everyone goes home. Is someone in charge of turning the heat down and making sure unnecessary lights are turned off at night? Are the heating and lighting on timers? Ask if the mechanical and electrical equipment in the school is in good operating condition. Do your own physical inspection of the school building. Ask yourself such questions as:

- Are there a lot of windows in the school? Are they on the side of the building that allows warm solar energy to come in during the winter? Are there shades to keep out the hot summer sun?
- What direction do the prevailing winds come from? Does the school building receive any protection from cold winds, as from other buildings or large trees?
- On windy or cold days, are there drafts around windows and outside doors?
- Are some rooms hotter than they need to be (in winter) or cooler than they need to be (in warm weather)? Use a thermometer to measure the temperature in rooms you feel are too warm or cold.
- Are there dripping or leaky faucets, or long or constantly flushing toilets

You need
- a custodian or maintenance person from your school
- a teacher
- a local builder or architect
- paper and pencil
- camera and film (optional)

in the rest rooms? Ask a friend of the opposite sex to help you check for such water waste.

- Is the water coming from the faucets so hot that it might scald someone? If so, the thermostat on the hot water heater may be set too high.
- Do the exhaust fans in the kitchen run unnecessarily?

Interview one or more teachers and ask them what they do to make their classroom more energy efficient. Do they store and use paper, books, and other materials wisely? Do the windows in their classrooms let in enough natural light so that the teacher can turn off some of the electric lights during the day? Are computers, printers, and other electronic equipment turned off when not in use? Interview a local builder or architect and ask for ideas on improving the energy efficiency of your school building.

Study the data you have collected and compile an energy report for your school. Include suggestions for improvement. Obviously, there will be some things you cannot change, such as the efficiency of the school's boiler. But you can ask teachers to assign a student to see that the lights are turned off when everyone leaves the room for recess or for lunch.

Most trash from schools is paper. Instead of throwing out paper that is only used on one side (old flyers and printed reports), ask teachers about making use of the other sides for scribbling notes or as scrap paper in classes. The school can also set up places where everyone can deposit used white paper for recycling.

You may want to enhance your report by taking photographs. Show and report on both good and bad points about your school building.

Project 46
WINDY CORNERS
Comparing available wind energy

Someday our homes may not need to be connected to electrical power lines for energy. Newly constructed or redesigned housing, with solar cells and efficient windmills, will perhaps in the future be able to gather energy and produce enough power to fill the needs of the families living there.

If you were thinking of installing a small windmill where you live, where around your house would be the best place to set it up? Usually, windmills are mounted very high up, in order to catch the strongest wind. But suppose you had to mount one on the ground. Where, on the ground, do you think the wind is strongest? Is it windier in the middle of the side wall of your house, or at the corners?

To find out, make a device to measure wind strength. Push a thumbtack into the eraser end of a pencil. Tie a piece of thread about 10 inches (25 cm) long onto the thumbtack.

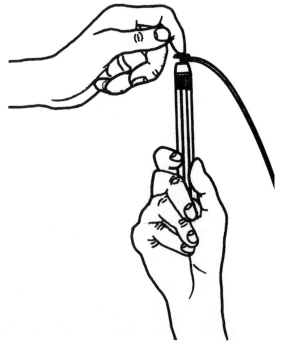

Make a sketch, or rough drawing, of the layout of your house, as it would be seen from overhead. On the drawing, label each side: A, B, C, and so on. Label each corner: 1, 2, 3, in the same way.

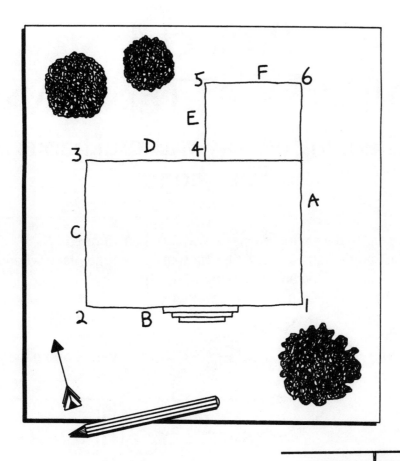

Go outside and stand in the middle of each side wall and at each corner of the house. At each position, hold the pencil straight up and at arm's length, to catch whatever wind there is. The windier it is, the greater the angle the thread will be from the pencil. Is it more windy along the broad sides of your house or at the corners?

Check the effect of the wind every day for a week (some days will be more windy than others). Is it true that the corners (or the sides) are always windier? Why do you think that is?

Project 47
ENERGY ATTENDANT
Changing energy-wasteful habits in your home

Can you help make saving energy a way of life for the people you live with? Using seat belts has become a good habit for many adults because their children nagged them every time they got into the car— the children having been taught about seat belt safety at school.

Before saving energy becomes a habit in your house, you will have to be on the alert for times when energy is being wasted and politely point it out to your family. Maybe you can change these energy-wasting patterns for the better, and make energy saving something your family does automatically, as routinely as getting up in the morning, eating breakfast, brushing teeth, and heading out for school or work.

Make a list of the ways your family can save energy, and give them a copy to remind them. Everyone should be happy to help, because they can all take part and saving energy will also save them money.

You need
- thge place where you live
- the people who live in your house or apartment
- pencil and paper

Some Simple Energy-Saving Ideas

- Before opening the refrigerator door, think about what you need. Then open the door, quickly get the items you want, and close the door. Every time a refrigerator door is open, heat from the room goes in, and the refrigerator must work to cool that warm air. It's a good idea to place often-used products (milk, eggs, butter, cheese) in the same place in the refrigerator so they can be found easily and time is not wasted searching.
- Turn off lights when a room is unoccupied.
- Televisions, computers, and radios should be turned off—*if* no one intends to use them within a half-hour. These appliances receive a lot of wear and tear when they are first turned on, so it's better to leave them on, for up to a half-hour, if you or someone will be using them within that time.
- Toast two slices of bread at the same time, instead of first one slice and then another a minute later. Toasters, like other electrical heating devices, use a lot of electricity.

Project 48
CHECK YOUR GAME
The energy cost of electronic fun

Before electricity was available in every home, families and friends entertained themselves by playing games using cards, boards, dice, "men," marbles, and other objects. With the invention of electricity and new advances in electronics, the world of games has really changed, with all kinds of computer and video games now filling store shelves.

Some games now available on home computer used to be played without using electrical energy. Card games like solitaire and board games like Monopoly, for example, are just two games now popular on computers that can still be played in the "traditional" way, saving energy.

How many games do you have that need energy to play them (don't forget battery-operated ones)? How many games do you own that do not require energy?

You need
<ul>
<li>pencil and paper</li>
<li>research</li>
<li>electric power company bil (optional)</li>
<li>television set, video computer game console, computer (optional)</li>
</ul>

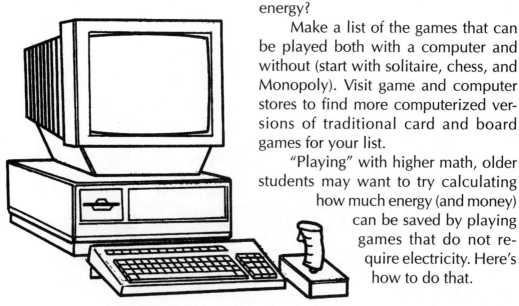

Make a list of the games that can be played both with a computer and without (start with solitaire, chess, and Monopoly). Visit game and computer stores to find more computerized versions of traditional card and board games for your list.

"Playing" with higher math, older students may want to try calculating how much energy (and money) can be saved by playing games that do not require electricity. Here's how to do that.

To determine the cost of using an electrical appliance, look for a label or tag on the unit or refer to the owner's manual to find its power consumption. The power consumption figure will be listed in "watts." Electric power companies charge by how many "kilowatt-hours" are used. One kilowatt is equal to 1,000 watts. It takes one kilowatt-hour of energy to operate ten 100-watt light bulbs for one hour (10 ´ 100 = 1,000).

To find out how much energy it takes to play a TV video game, look on the back of the television set and on the video game console for the power consumption of each, listed in "watts." Add the two numbers together. Let's assume that the video game uses 50 watts and the television set uses 150 watts. That makes a total of 200 watts. To convert this to "kilowatts," a unit the power company uses, divide 200 by 1,000, which equals 0.200 kilowatts. Have an adult search out a recent electric bill and help you determine how much it costs for 1 kilowatt-hour of power. You can get a rough idea by dividing the amount due on the electric bill by the number of kilowatt-hours used that month. This information will be listed on the electric bill.

Suppose your electric bill was $165.13 and the kilowatt-hours used was 1,365. Dividing $165.13 by 1,365 equals 0.12, or 12 cents per kilowatt-hour. So, to play the video game for one hour would cost about 0.200 times 12 cents, or 2.4 cents. It may not sound like much money, but just think of how many hours a year you and your family spend playing that video game! Calculate how much it does cost you for a year!

To find how much energy it takes to play a computer game, remember to add the power consumption of both the CPU (the "central processing unit," or main part of the computer) and the monitor, since both are needed.

Project 49
HEAT WAVE

Discovering how microwaves generate heat

Microwaves are a kind of radio frequency energy (electromagnetic waves). Their frequency (the number of times the wave vibrates each second) is much higher than most other types of radio and TV waves.

Microwaves are used for telephone and satellite communications, and for fast cooking. When microwaves pass through food, they cause the molecules in the food to move back and forth very rapidly. This generates heat. Have you ever rubbed your hands together rapidly to warm them? A microwave oven works in a similar way. Microwaves vibrate the molecules of water, sugar and fat in food, but pass right through glass, pottery, paper, wood and plastic. That is why, although food cooks in a microwave oven, the dish doesn't get hot—except for some heat transfer from the food. Metal blocks microwaves, so should never be used in a microwave oven.

Can you prove that a microwave oven does not cook by making the air in the oven hot, like a traditional oven does, but by heating up the food from the inside? Ask an adult to help, and fill a cup with water. Put it inside a microwave oven and heat it for 60 seconds. Be sure the cup is "microwave safe," that is, made of plastic, glass or pottery without any metal in it or metallic decorations on it.

When the time is up, take the cup out of the oven. Lay a thermometer inside the oven and close the door (but DO NOT turn the oven on). Stick a thermometer into the cup of water. After about two minutes, take the thermometer out of the oven and compare it to the one from the cup of water. Does the thermometer that was in the water read a higher temperature than the one placed in the oven?

You need
- use of microwave oven
- 2 thermometers
- pencils
- coffee or tea cup (must be "microwave safe")
- water
- an adult

Project 50
NO TAN WANTED
Cold-blooded animals and heat energy

Animals gather energy from the sun to warm their bodies and maintain their normal life pro-cesses. Even turtles, which are cold-blooded animals, sit for hours on rocks along a pond "sunning" themselves. A captive snake is sometimes seen standing straight up. It does this to get more light on its body to warm it-

You need
- books, photographs, and other research materials
- arts and crafts supplies

self. Iguanas need heat to properly digest their food. Grasshoppers cannot chirp if the temperature falls below 62 degrees Fahrenheit (17 degrees Celsius).

Research cold-blooded animals that must have warming energy from the sun in order to live. Draw or construct a scene showing how these various animals gather warmth from the sun.

Project 51
STATIC INTERFERENCE
Detecting sources of stray radio frequency energy

One kind of energy that we can't see or hear is called radio frequency energy. Radio frequency energy is formed by electromagnetic waves that travel through the air. Radio frequency energy allows us to communicate with one another. It is used to bring TV pictures and sound to our homes from stations far away. Two-way radios let people talk to each other from remote places (you may even own a pair of "walkie talkies"). Cordless telephones allow people to talk on the phone while walking around the house or going

You need
- electric shaver
- cordless telephone
- fluorescent light
- electric blanket
- electric hair dryer
- AM radio
- personal computer
- television
- paper and pencil

outside without being restricted by a wire connecting the handset to the telephone base. "Cellular phones," both hand-held and car phones, permit communications with people who are not near a regular telephone. All of these types of communication are possible because of an invisible kind of energy called radio frequency energy.

Some things may give off radio frequency energy, even when we don't want them to. Things that have electric motors often produce radio frequency energy when they are working. This energy may be unwanted, since it can interfere with other things that use radio frequencies, such as TVs, radios, and cordless telephones.

What things around your home do you think might be radiating (giving off) radio frequency energy? How about an electric shaver, a fluorescent light, an electric blanket, an electric hair dryer, an AM radio, a personal computer, or a television?

Since we cannot see or hear radio frequency energy, we will use a radio as a detector to help us find things around the house that are producing radio frequency energy.

Tune a portable AM radio to a spot on the dial where no station is heard. Bring the radio close to each of these objects:

- an electric shaver
- a fluorescent light (often found in the kitchen or bathroom)
- an electric blanket
- an electric hair dryer
- a personal computer
- a television (turn the volume down on the TV set)

Write down your observations about each appliance. Did you hear a sound in the radio? If so, describe the sound; was it a crackling sound or a humming sound?

Call a friend on a cordless telephone. Ask your friend to be quiet and listen. Then hold your phone close to each of the appliances listed above, asking your friend each time what she or he hears, if anything. If your friend has a cordless phone, it's your turn to listen. What do you hear?

What other things around your home or school can you check out as radio frequency producers? What do you think—which makes the better radio frequency detector, an AM radio, or a cordless telephone?

Project 52
GREAT BARRIER ICE
Magnetism versus water and ice

Magnetism, an invisible form of energy, can go through air. Can it go through water? What if the water is in the form of ice, where the molecules are in a more orderly and structured form. Does it affect magnetism?

Fill a long, cylindrically shaped balloon with water. Don't inflate the balloon, just fill it with water in its uninflated shape. Tie the balloon to the middle of a pencil. Lay the pencil across two cups or glasses to let the balloon hang down. Lay a book on either side of the cups, so that they are separated by the balloon. On one book place a staple, and on the other, a strong magnet.

With the water-filled balloon between the staple and magnet, move staple and/or magnet until they are just close enough to each other that the staple is captured by the magnetic force of

the magnet. Note the spot where the staple first showed signs of being attracted by the magnet. Measure the distance between the magnet and this spot.

Without disturbing the books or the magnet, move the cups, with the pencil and balloon in place, to the freezer. Keep the setup the same, so the balloon will have the same shape as when the ice was water. When the water in the balloon has frozen, remove the setup from the freezer and put it back by the books.

Place the staple back on the book opposite the magnet at the spot where it was first attracted to the magnet. Does the force of magnetism go through the ice and move the staple? If it does, is there any difference in the distance between the staple and the magnet before the magnetic attraction affects the staple?

You need
• strong magnet
• staple, from stapler
• 2 cups or glasses
• 2 books
• pencil
• cylindrically-shaped balloon
• use of a freezer
• ruler

Project 53
ONWARD & UPWARD
Transfering energy uphill

Can a wave of energy travel uphill? We learned, in Project 25, that energy travels in the form of a wave, and moves forward even though the objects passing the energy along do not. (They *may* move, but only a short distance compared to that of the energy transferred.) But uphill…?

You need
• ruler
• dominoes

Place two dominos under a ruler to make a sloping ramp. Stand a domino on the ruler with its broad sides facing the ends. If the standing domino falls over, remove a domino under the ruler. If it stays standing, try to add another domino to make the ramp even steeper. Add dominos under the ruler until the ramp is as steep as possible without the upright standing dominos on top falling over. When you have made the ramp as steep as you can, stand a line of dominos along the ramp. Space them about 1 inch (2 cm) apart.

Push on the top half of the first domino, on the lowest part of the ramp, and tip it forward into the next-higher one. Does a chain reaction occur and knock the top domino off the ruler? If so, a wave of energy, which came from your "push," traveled uphill, even though the actual domino you pushed only moved a little bit.

To do more experimenting with this project, you may want to try making a wave of energy go even more steeply uphill. You can do this by building steps with building blocks, or other materials, and again using dominos to try to transfer the energy uphill. With steps, the dominos can stand on a level surface; but remember that to make the next domino in line fall forward, it must be hit on its top half. If it is struck near the middle or its lower half, it could fall backwards instead of forward.

Project 54
INVISIBLE BEAMS
Locating light in the darkness

Some kinds of energy are invisible. A beam of light energy itself is invisible. We see light only when the light energy directly enters the eye, or reflects off an object and bounces into the eye.

Normally, we can't see the light rays that are coming from the sun *(never look directly at the sun)* but only see the things the sunlight shines on. At dusk, after the sun has set where you are, you may have noticed the sun's light shining brightly on an airplane flying overhead. High in the sky, the airplane is still being hit by the sun's light energy rays, even though you can no longer see the sun from Earth's surface.

You may also have seen sunbeams, when the sun's light streams through a break in the clouds. Because there are billions of tiny dust particles in the air, it's possible to see the sun's light energy bouncing off them against a dark sky

> **You need**
> - flashlight
> - small cardboard box
> - scissors
> - talcum powder
> - a dark room
> - an adult

86

beyond. Other times, after a rainstorm, the water droplets in the atmosphere behind us, away from the setting sun, will reflect the sun's light at different angles and show you a rainbow. Sunlight also contains other types of invisible energy rays that we cannot see. In the summer, you cannot see the ultraviolet rays coming from the sun, but too much of this kind of energy will give you a sunburn!

To make light rays visible, have an adult help you cut a small hole about the size of a large coin in a small cardboard box (a shoebox would work well). Turn a flashlight on and place it inside the box so that its light shines out through the hole. Close up the box so that the hole is the only place where light can escape from inside.

Place the box on a table or dresser in a very dark room. Standing several feet in front of the box, gently shake or squeeze some talcum powder from its container into range of the light energy coming out of the box. The light from the flashlight in the box can now be seen bouncing from the powdery talcum particles.

A light beam can also be a useful tool, helping us to see particles in the air that are normally too small for us to notice or see well. Instead of using talcum powder, if you have them try clapping two chalkboard erasers together. You can also shake a fresh facial tissue, right from a box, into the beam. Try different brands of facial tissue. Do some give off more lint particles than others?

Project 55
PENNY SHOOT
Newton's law and the transfer of energy

Sir Isaac Newton, an early scientist born in England in 1642, formulated the physics laws of motion. His first law of motion states that "an object at rest tends to stay at rest, and an object in motion tends to stay in motion." A famous trick demonstrates this law. A playing card is placed over a drinking cup and a coin is laid on top of the card, directly over the mouth of the cup. Then the edge of the card is given a sharp tap with a finger or pencil.

The blow knocks the card off the cup, but the coin on the card, being at rest, stays in position. Then gravity pulls down on the coin and it drops into the cup.

Let's build a device that will not only demonstrate this law of Newton's, but also show transfer of energy (energy from one object being handed off to another object).

Cut a strip of smooth paper to fit on the wooden board. Towards one end of the board, hammer two small nails, spaced about 3 inches (7.5 cm) apart, partway into the wood. The nails should be sticking up out of the wood about an inch (2.5 cm), looking like goal posts at a football field. Stretch a small rubber band between the two "goal post" nails. Cut a small strip of thin cardboard, about an inch (2.5 cm) wide by two inches (5 cm) long. Fold it in half around the rubber band (in the middle) and staple the cardboard ends together. Push the rubber band down on the goal posts, so it rests almost against the wood.

About one inch (2.5 cm) in front of the goal posts, place one of the medium coins face up. Then stack four more of the coins on top, but with tails up.

Grab the stapled piece of folded cardboard between your thumb and index finger and pull back. A stretched rubber band is said to have "potential energy," energy that is stored up and ready to do work.

While the rubber band is stretched, place the smaller coin between the goal posts. Release the cardboard so that it strikes this coin and shoots it towards the stack. The idea is to knock the bottom coin out from under, leaving the other four stacked coins at rest (although they will drop straight down due to gravity).

You may have to try this several times. Your aim may be off, and sometimes the smaller coin may fly slightly upwards and miss hitting the bottom nickel. If a coin does move from the stack, it may happen too fast for you to see. To be sure it was the bottom coin that really was knocked out, see if the coin that was moved has heads or tails up. If it's heads, then you successfully shot out the bottom nickel.

This project also shows two examples of the transfer of energy. When the stretched rubber band (potential energy) is released (kinetic energy), energy from the rubber band is transferred to the smaller coin, giving it motion. Energy is then transferred again when this coin hits the stacked coins. The force must be great enough for this struck coin to overcome the friction of the coins on top of it—and the surface under it, which is why we placed a piece of smooth paper under the stack.

The "momentum" of the moving coin will determine just how far it will travel after it has been shot out from under the pile. Remember, "objects in motion tend to stay in motion," so once the nickel is moving, it will *naturally* try to keep going; friction eventually slows it down enough to make it stop.

FLIGHT, SPACE
&ASTRONOMY

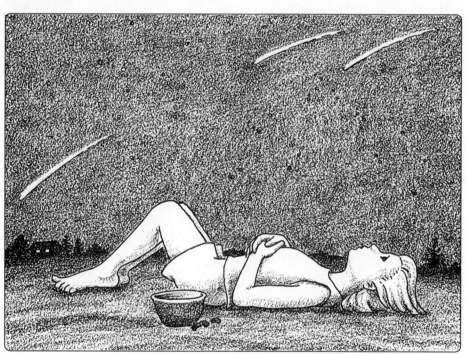

A Note to the Parent

People have always looked up at the sky and the things in it with awe and wonder. That fascination creates an exciting desire to learn about our universe. The world we see above and around us is a unique part of our environment.

This book provides a selection of science projects about flight, astronomy and space. It offers a blend of many science disciplines: math, physics, aerodynamics, optics and astronomy. The concepts presented include: devices that move through the air, air pressure, lighter-than-air objects, lunar calendars and phases, constellations, solar effects, and much more. Your young people will work with kites, parachutes, balloons, bubbles, compasses, binoculars and telescopes to learn about science.

Science should be enjoyable, interesting and thought-provoking—that is the concept the writers wish to convey. While this book presents many scientific ideas and learning techniques that are valuable and useful, the approach is designed to entice the child with the excitement and fun of scientific investigation.

The material is presented in a light and interesting fashion. For example, the concept of measurement can be demonstrated by teaching precise measuring in inches or centimeters, or by having a child stretch his or her arms around a tree trunk and asking, "Are all children's reaches the same?" We present science in a way that does not seem like science.

The scientific concepts introduced here will form a basis to help the young student later understand more advanced scientific principles. Projects will develop those science skills needed in our ever increasingly complex society: skills such as classifying objects, making measured observations, thinking clearly and accurately recording data. Values are dealt with in a general way. One should never harm any living thing just for the sake of it. Respect for life should be fundamental. Disruption of natural processes should not occur thoughtlessly and unnecessarily. Interference with ecological systems should always be avoided.

Project 56
WHO'S IN THE MOON?
Imagination and moon images

Have you ever heard anyone talk about the Man in the Moon? Some people say that, when they look up at the moon, they see a face looking down. Long ago, some ancient peoples feared the power of the moon, while others worshiped it and were happy that the moon kept watch at night.

You need
- clear evening with a full moon
- pencil and paper
- clipboard (optional)

When you look up at the moon from Earth, the light and dark patterns you see there can form shapes. Today we know, because we have been there and seen the moon's surface close up, that those light and dark patterns are the mountains, giant craters and waterless seas on the moon. We have even mapped the moon's surface in great detail.

On an evening when the moon is full, take a pad or a clipboard with paper and draw the shapes you see. Then use your imagination. Can you see a face in the shapes you have drawn?

If so, is it the face of a man or woman, or do you see a boy, a girl or some sort of animal?

Just as the ancient people used their imaginations to see creatures in the patterns of the stars, use your imagination to fill in details of your "Face in the Moon," adding ears, hair, a body shape and anything else you see. Give the figure a name and write a story telling who it is and how it came to be in the moon.

Project 57
"THREE, TWO, ONE..."
A matter of action and reaction

"For every action there is an equal and opposite reaction." This law of physics was first discovered by Sir Isaac Newton in 1687. Suppose you and your friend are both wearing roller skates and your friend is standing in front of you. If you push him, he will roll away in the direction of your push, but you will roll, too. A force that is equal but opposite acts to push you backwards!

Gases or liquids are sometimes pushed through an opening to move, or propel, an object forward. This principle is called "jet propulsion." This is how jet airplanes, missiles and rockets move through the air and even maneuver in outer space.

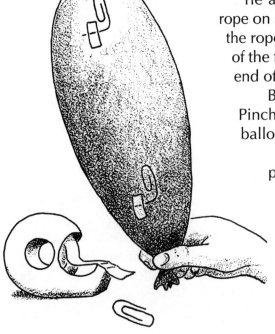

Tie a piece of string or fishing line to the rope on a flagpole used to raise a flag. Pull on the rope so that the string is pulled to the top of the flagpole. Have a friend hold the other end of the string.

Blow up an oblong-shaped balloon. Pinch the neck to keep the air inside the balloon.

Have your friend bend one end of a paper clip to form an "L" shape. Bend a second paper clip the same way.

Using sticky tape, fasten the L-shape leg of both paper clips onto the same side of the balloon, one near the neck end that you are holding and the other near the closed end. Hook both paper clips onto the string on the flagpole so that the balloon's neck is towards you.

The string should be pulled tight by your friend and kept straight. Let go of the balloon's neck. Rushing to escape, the air inside the balloon will push against the inside front wall and the balloon will shoot straight up along the string like a rocket.

How high do you think it will go? Is the force of gravity stronger than the force of the escaping air that pushes the balloon forward, or will the balloon continue to shoot upward until it runs out of air?

What kind of path would the balloon take if you didn't have it on a string to keep it going in a straight line? If you used a shorter rod, say about three feet (90 cm) in length, instead of a long string, would the balloon continue on in a straight line after it left the end of the rod?

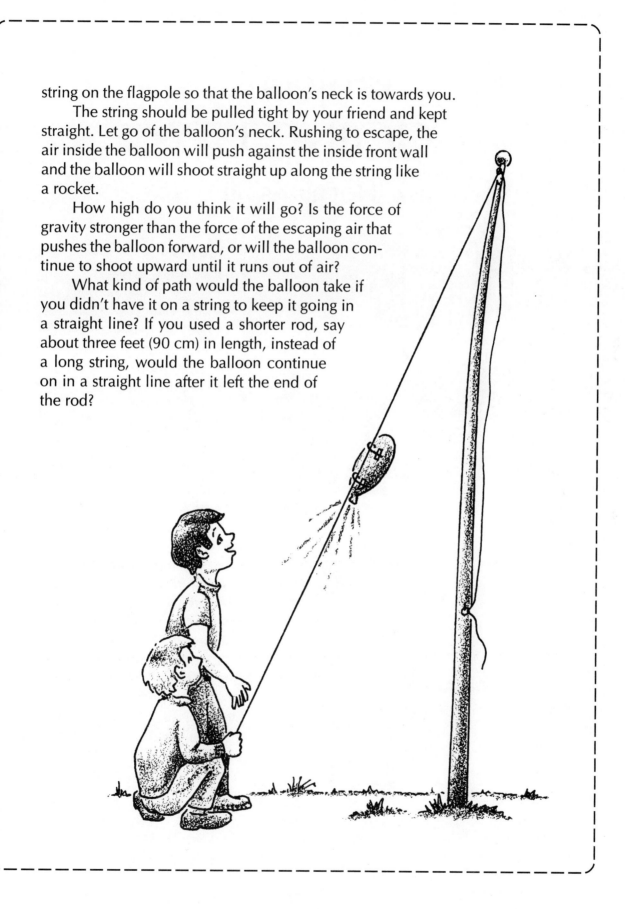

Project 58
GOING UP?

Hot air rising

You need
- glycerin
- water
- pipe cleaner
- use of a toaster
- small bowl
- liquid soap
- kitchen measuring cup
- tablespoon
- an adult

Hot air rises, which is partially the cause of tornadoes and other weather conditions.

In June of 1783, in France, a large bag made of paper was filled with hot air and smoke from a fire. The bag floated up to about 6,000 feet. It was the beginning of hot-air balloons, used today to carry weather instruments high above the Earth, and the popular sport of hot-air ballooning. Your challenge: prove that hot air rises.

You will need some bubble solution, either bought or home-made. To make your own bubble solution, pour $\frac{1}{2}$ measuring cup of water into a bowl. Add $\frac{1}{4}$ cup of liquid soap, such as dishwashing detergent or liquid hand soap. Have an adult measure out and add one tablespoon of glycerin. (Glycerin should be handled carefully, and by an adult. You must not get any in your mouth, or place the glycerin near anything hot—because it can catch fire.) Use the tablespoon to stir your solution.

If a bubble wand didn't come with the bought solution, make one by bending one end of a pipe cleaner into a circle about the size of a large coin or bottle cap.

On a table or countertop, have an adult plug in a toaster and push down the handle, as if to toast a slice of bread. Be very careful, because toasters get very hot. Keep the bubble solution—in fact, any liquids—away from the toaster.

Dip the wand into your bubble solution. Stand about two to three feet (60-90 cm) away from the toaster. Slowly, blow into the wand, aiming bubbles across the top of the hot toaster. What happens to the bubbles as they float over the heated toaster?

Are there other places in your home where you might detect rising hot air by the bubble method?

Project 59
MOON WATCH
Discovering the moon's motions

Our moon is always moving in the sky. It takes the moon about 27$\frac{1}{3}$ days to make one orbit around the Earth. The moon moves across the sky not only because the Earth is turning beneath it, but because the moon is orbiting the Earth.

From your local newspaper, a calendar or an almanac, find out when the next full moon will be. The moon will look full for several days.

You need
- modeling clay
- cardboard paper towel roll
- window with view of moon
- clear evenings near time of full moon
- full moon timetable from almanac or newspaper
- table
- clock
- cardboard about 1 foot (13 cm) square
- pencil and paper

Find a window where you can look out in the early evening and see the moon. Use a wide windowsill or move a small table or other surface to the window. Place a piece of cardboard on it to keep it clean. Put some modeling clay on it and mold the clay to be able to hold the cardboard tube from a paper towel roll. The tube will need to be held in place at an angle at the edge of the sill or table in order for you to look through it.

When the full moon can be seen in the window, look through the tube and move it until the moon is centered in it. Mold the clay around the tube to keep it in place without anyone needing to hold it. Look at a clock. Write down the exact time. Be sure no one in your house touches the tube for the next few days.

The next night, look through the tube again at exactly the exact same time as you did the night before. Is the moon still seen in the middle of the tube?

For the next several nights, look through the tube at exactly the same time. Where is the moon? Is it getting higher in the sky each evening, lower in the sky, or is it in the exact same spot? On paper, draw how much of the moon you see through the tube each night.

Project 60
DOUBLE DIPPER
Seeing star patterns

To help keep track of the many stars in the sky, the ancient Greeks grouped stars together into patterns. These groups of stars are called constellations. The ancient peoples also gave the constellations names, but today we find it hard to recognize the strange creatures they saw when they looked at the night sky.

You need
- pencil and paper
- some newspaper
- use of a copy machine
- a few friends

The Big Dipper, or The Ladle, in the northern sky is a popular name for a constellation which really does look like a big spoon. The stars that make up the shape of the Big Dipper are part of the constellation the ancients called Ursa Major, which means Great Bear. Can you find the Big Dipper tonight? Can you see other patterns in the sky? Do other people see the same stars that you do? Do you think they see the same patterns in the sky that you do, too?

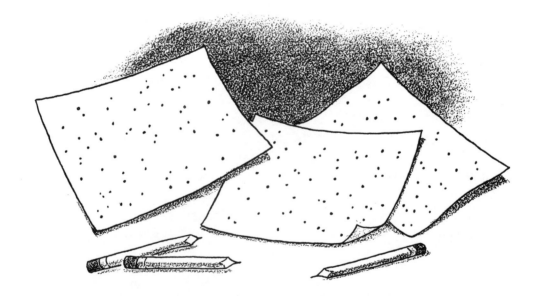

Place some newspaper on a table to protect it from being marked up. Take a sheet of white paper, put it on the newspaper and, with your eyes closed, make about 50 dots all over the paper. To be sure that you are making the dots at random, not in any special pattern, you might want to have a friend slide the paper around a little while you are making the dots. When you are done, take the pencil and make each dot you made a little bigger, so they are easier to see.

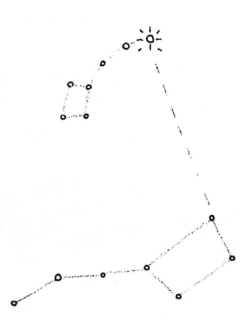

Using a copy machine, make 5 copies of your dotted paper.

Taking one of the copies, study the dots. Try to find patterns that look like capital letters of the alphabet and connect some of the dots to make them.

Give one of the other four copies to each of your parents or some of your friends. Don't let them see your copy with the letter shapes on it. Ask them to make as many capital letters as they can by connecting the dots.

Do you think they will see the same patterns in your random dots that you did?

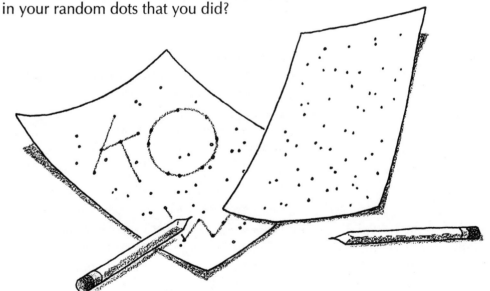

Project 61
SUPER-SIZE SURPRISE
Sunlight from two directions

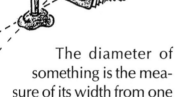

You need
- pencil
- sheet of typing paper
- book
- ruler
- clothespin or clay
- 2 flashlights

The diameter of something is the measure of its width from one side to the other. The sun is very far away, but it is so large that its diameter sends a wide path of sunlight to us, from both sides of the sun's diameter and everywhere in between.

It even seems as if the light is coming from more than one place, because the wide path of sunlight makes things have more than one shadow.

Go outside on a sunny day. Place a sheet of paper on the ground and put a pencil on it. Slowly move the pencil upward. As you raise the pencil above the paper, you will begin to see two shadows. The higher you go, the harder it is to see each shadow. As the light from one side of the sun causes a pencil shadow, it also washes out the pencil shadow caused by the light coming from the other side of the sun's diameter.

Do this little experiment using two flashlights to see how the light coming from each side of the sun is like having two different sources of light. Take the sheet of typing paper and tape it to the side of a book. Open the book a little bit and set it on a table so that the open part faces down. It will look like a movie screen. Use a clothespin or some clay to hold your pencil straight up in the air. Place the pencil about 6 inches (15 cm) in front of the book. Put two flashlights on the table, about 18 inches (45 cm) in front of the book. Turn on one of the flashlights. Point the light at the pencil to make a shadow on the paper screen. Now turn on the second flashlight and point it at the pencil. It will make a shadow of the pencil, too. But see how the light also washes out the first shadow, making it fainter.

Project 62
CYCLOPS
Two light sources into one

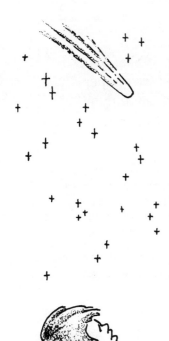

What a shock it was, back in 1609, when Galileo invented the first practical telescope! Through this amazing instrument, people were able to see things in the night sky that they could never see before.

You need
- a cardboard box, 2 or 3 (60 or 90 cm) high
- 2 flashlights
- a clear evening, at dusk

When we look at the sky using only our eyes, almost all we see are just tiny points of light, some brighter, some fainter. But those points of light are really much more than that. With telescopes we can see that one of the points of light is a nearby planet, Saturn, that has rings around it. Big telescopes can see strange cloud-like shapes called nebulae. What looks like just one point of light might actually be two stars, or perhaps even thousands of stars, but without a telescope, we would never know it.

You can prove that it is possible for two sources of light to look like only one. Go outside just before nightfall. Stand a cardboard box on the ground. A sidewalk is good place to set your box. On top of the box place two flashlights side by side. Make sure they are both pointing straight ahead. How far do you have to walk away from the box before the two lights look like just one?

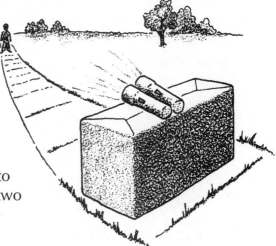

Project 63
HIGH FLYER

Designing paper airplanes for distance

In paper-airplane design, the goal is a plane that will stay in the air a long time before gravity pulls it down. Does wing shape make a difference? What about the material used to make the plane?

Make three paper airplanes using the same design. Instructions for a popular basic design are given on the opposite page, or you can use one of your own. Make one plane using regular paper, one out of aluminum foil, and one out of wax paper. Which plane stays in the air the longest?

Experiment with different airplane designs using the three different types of material. A design that works best for the aluminum plane might not work well for the plane made out of wax paper.

Experiment with different ways of keeping the plane together. Try putting a small bit of flattened tacky clay in the fold at the front. Try placing a paper clip on the bottom of the plane, near its middle. Try putting a piece of light tape on the plane's nose, or across its wingspan.

Do the planes fly better when there is a wind? Should you launch the planes into the wind, or with the wind behind you? Do you get better flights if you just toss the planes easily, or if you throw them harder, trying to make them go farther?

Make a chart of your flight tests and compare the results.

> **You need**
> • sheet of typing paper
> • piece of wax paper
> • piece of aluminum foil
> • adhesive tape
> • paper clips
> • tacky clay

Design for Basic Paper Airplane

1. Fold a sheet of typing paper in half lengthwise and crease it.
2. Open up and flatten the sheet.
3. At one end, fold both corners down, lining edges up with the center crease.
4. Fold each corner edge down again, against the center fold, and crease well. Fold in the sharp point, for safety when tossing.
5. Turn the paper over.
6. Fold the two outer edges back into the creased center line.
7. Fold the plane together and crease all folds well.
8. Bend the wings out into position and test fly your plane.

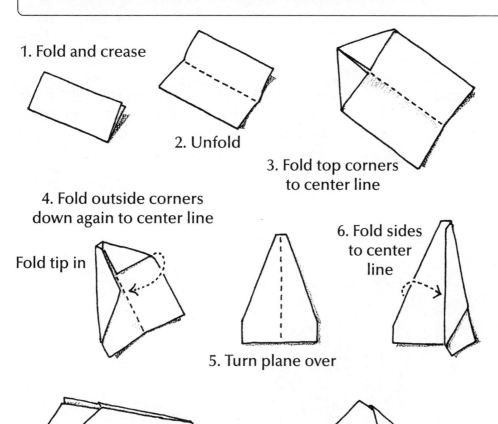

1. Fold and crease

2. Unfold

3. Fold top corners to center line

4. Fold outside corners down again to center line

Fold tip in

5. Turn plane over

6. Fold sides to center line

7. Fold plane flat and crease all folds

8. Open out wings... and fly!

Project 64
NEWS FLASH
Naming comets

Many comets are discovered by "backyard astronomers," amateurs who enjoy looking at and studying the stars. When a new comet is discovered, it is given the designation of the year and a letter indicating the number of comets that year. For example, comet 1997b would be the second comet discovered in 1997. Later, the comet is given the name of the person who first discovered it (sometimes two or three people's names are used).

> **You need**
> • pencil and paper

Make believe you discovered a comet. How would you describe it and report its location? What constellation was it in? What star was it near? How bright was it? What time did you discover it? Where were you when you saw it? How long did you watch? What direction was it going? Be as exact as you can.

Write a pretend press release telling the story of your discovery.

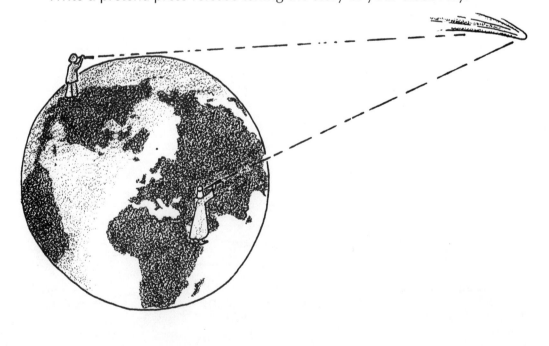

Project 65
OVERCOMING GRAVITY
Countering one force with another

What is keeping you from floating up into the air right now? It's gravity. All of the planets and the stars have a force, called gravity, that pulls things to them. If you hold something heavy in your hand and hold your arm out straight, you can feel how strong the Earth's gravity is, as it tries to pull your arm downward. But if you know how, you can make an ordinary paper clip defy gravity. Your friends will think you are a magician when they see it floating in midair.

You need
- shoe box
- thread
- magnet
- construction paper
- adhesive tape
- paper clip
- crayons

The secret is magnetism, a force that can be stronger than gravity. To defy gravity, tape a strong magnet inside one end of the shoe box. Use construction paper and crayons to decorate the "magic" box, hiding the magnet so your friends can't see it. Stand the shoe box up on the end without the magnet. Tie a piece of thread to a small paper clip. Hold one end of the thread on the inside bottom of the shoe box. Slowly pull the paper clip up towards the magnet, letting the thread out. At the point where the paper clip will stay in the air by itself, tape the section of string touching the bottom to the box. Then pull the clip down, away from the magnet. When your friends come over, slowly lift the paper clip up towards the top of the box and let go when it stands up by itself. Abracadabra!

Project 66
A BALANCED DIET
Gravity and the balancing point

The attraction objects have for each other is called gravity. Gravity keeps the planets orbiting around the sun, and keeps the moon orbiting around the Earth. The Earth's gravity pulls things down to it.

Have you ever balanced a long pole on your shoulder? Your shoulder was the resting point on which you balanced it. What part did you rest on your shoulder? Was it about at the middle of the pole?

Try balancing a spoon on your finger. Where is the balancing point?

Push the teeth of the two forks together. This new object now has a balancing point that is in midair! You can prove this by pushing a flat stick through the teeth of the forks and resting the middle of the stick on the edge of a coffee cup.

Stand with your back up against a wall and with your heels touching it. Try to bend down and touch your toes while keeping your heels touching the

You need
- 12-inch (30 cm) ruler
- about 10 pennies
- pencil with flat sides
- table

wall. As you start to lean forward, your balancing point changes. It is no longer a point that is over your feet, and you will fall forward.

If an object, like a long pole, is just as heavy on one side as it is the other, the balancing point should be in the middle. But where is the balancing point if one side has more weight?

Lay a pencil on a table. Use a pencil which has flat sides to keep it from rolling. Place a ruler

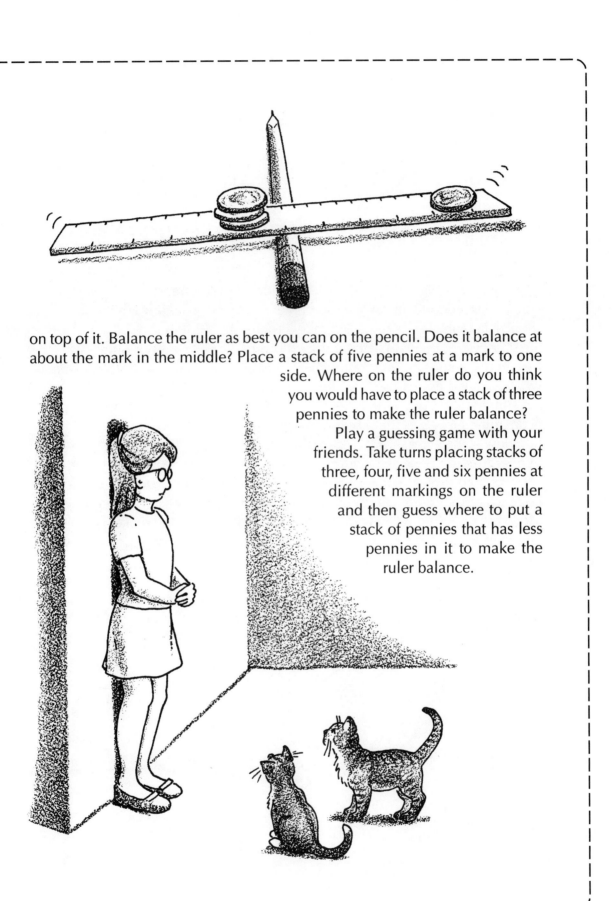

on top of it. Balance the ruler as best you can on the pencil. Does it balance at about the mark in the middle? Place a stack of five pennies at a mark to one side. Where on the ruler do you think you would have to place a stack of three pennies to make the ruler balance?

Play a guessing game with your friends. Take turns placing stacks of three, four, five and six pennies at different markings on the ruler and then guess where to put a stack of pennies that has less pennies in it to make the ruler balance.

Project 67
BIG MONEY
Take a coin, cause an eclipse

The sun is very big. Its diameter (the distance across it) is 865,000 miles! The moon is much smaller. Its diameter is only 2,160 miles. There are times when the path of the moon brings it between the sun and the Earth. This causes what is called an eclipse. The moon blocks the sun and the sky goes dark even though it is daytime. How can the tiny moon blot out our view of the giant sun? It happens because things close to you look bigger than when they are farther away.

You can prove this by holding a coin out in front of you at arm's length. Look up at the moon on an evening when the moon is full. Close one eye. Move the nickel between your eye and the moon. Does the nickel blot out the whole moon? (Don't use the sun for this project! Never look directly towards the sun or you can hurt your eyes.)

Next, hold a measuring stick vertically (up and down) at arm's length. Look at a telephone pole down the street. Close one eye. Move the ruler between your eye and the telephone pole. Does the ruler blot out the whole telephone pole?

Project 68
ROLLING ALONG
Demonstrating gravity's effect on light

A force is something that causes a change in something else. The force of gravity stops our motion upward when we jump. The gravity of the sun is so strong that it has trapped the Earth and other planets and keeps them all orbiting around it. The grav-

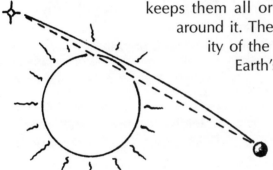

You need
- pea-sized steel ball bearing
- strong magnet
- flat table

ity of the moon is so strong that it pulls on the Earth's oceans and causes the tides.

The sun is so large that the force of its gravity can even change the path of light. Scientists report being able to see stars that are actually a little behind the edge of the sun. This is because the sun's gravity *bends* the stars' light around the edge. (Remember, never look directly at the sun, or you can hurt your eyes.)

Magnetic force is much the same. You can demonstrate how the force of gravity bends the path of light by using a strong magnet and a steel ball bearing. You might be able to get a ball bearing from your school science teacher, a hobby shop, or a bicycle or machine shop. A TV repair shop is good place to find a strong magnet. An adult could help you remove the magnet from an old speaker.

Roll a ball bearing slowly across a flat tabletop. It should roll in a straight line. Now place the magnet very close to the path where you rolled the ball bearing. Roll it again. Does the path of the ball bearing change as it passes by the magnet?

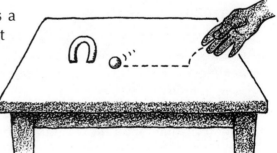

Project 69
SKYWORKS
All out for meteor spotting

Did you ever see a shooting star? Some people also call them falling stars, but their scientific name is meteors. A meteor is something—a piece of ice or rock—that has been traveling through space and enters the Earth's atmosphere. Some meteors are as tiny as a grain of sand, others are much larger. These meteors are moving so fast that heat caused by friction with the Earth's atmosphere burns them up. That's why we see them in the night sky as bright streaks of light.

You need
- a clear, dark night on one of the evenings listed on the chart on opposite page
- bag of dry navy beans
- bowl
- clock or watch

Some meteors are too big to burn up completely, so they hit the Earth's surface. The meteors that hit the Earth are called meteorites. Don't worry about being hit by one. Only about 18 meteorites are found each year, and that includes those that may have fallen ages ago and are only recently discovered.

On any dark, clear night you can usually see a few meteors if you are patient enough and watch closely. At certain times, though, you have a much better chance of seeing lots of them. This is when there is a meteor shower. Some popular meteor showers even have names, and people watch for them at about the same time every year. This is because the Earth moves through the same part of space, and the same clumps of tiny space particles, every year as it orbits the sun.

Scientists aren't sure where all of the meteor shower particles come from. The Taurids shower, which occurs around November 4 every year, is believed to be ice particles from the "tail" of Encke's Comet, and maybe little pieces of the comet head itself. Some meteors could be parts of a broken-up asteroid, or even pieces of the surface of the moon or Mars that were shot up into space during a collision.

On a dark, clear night, go outside and watch for meteors. You may want to put a blanket and pillow on the ground and lie on your back, or lie on an

Annual Meteor Showers	
Approximate Date	**Shower Name**
January 3	Quadrantids
April 21	Lyrids
May 4	Eta Aquarids
August 12	Perseids
October 10	Draconids
October 21	Orionids
November 4	Taurids
November 14	Androme

outdoor lounge chair so you can look up at the sky. Dress appropriately for the weather. If the date is close to one of the annual meteor showers (listed on the Annual Meteor Showers chart), take a bag of dry navy beans and bowl outside with you. Watch the sky for one hour. Keep a few beans in your hand. Every time you see a meteor, drop a bean into the bowl. At the end of the hour, count the beans in the bowl to find out how many meteors you saw. By using beans in order to count the meteors that you see, instead of using a pencil and paper, you don't have to take your eyes off the sky or use any light.

Learn more about meteors and meteorites at your local library or science center.

Project 70
MARBLE SLIDE
Trajectory trials

The path an object takes as it travels through the air is called its trajectory. The Earth's gravity pulls on everything. If you throw an object, it will not go straight. Soon it falls to the ground. The harder you throw it, the farther it will go before it hits the ground, but it will still hit the ground eventually. It is gravity that keeps you from being able to throw a baseball into space, no matter how good you can throw.

You need
- modeling clay
- tube from a paper towel roll
- marble
- several sheets of typing paper
- adhesive tape
- pencil
- cardboard
- an uncarpeted floor under the table

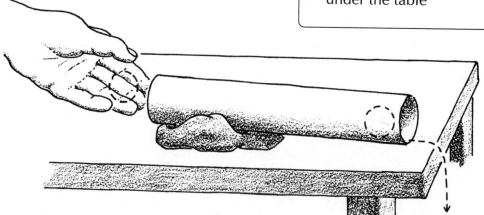

Let's play a guessing game about the trajectory of a marble rolling off a table. Put some cardboard on a table to protect it. Place a mound of modeling clay on the cardboard and make a marble slide by laying the tube against the mound so that the lower end is just slightly off the table. The slope or angle of the tube slide should be very small, that is, the higher end of the tube only a little higher than the lower end.

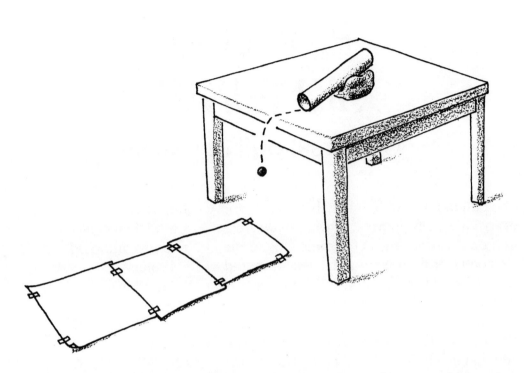

Take three or four sheets of typing paper and tape them together, end to end, making one long piece of paper a yard or so long (90 cm). Put the paper on the floor under the edge of the table below the marble slide. Tape the paper to the floor so it won't move.

Hold a marble at the raised end of the slide. Let it go. (Don't push it at all. Let the marble roll on its own.) As the marble rolls off the edge of the table, watch where it hits the floor. Mark the landing spot on the paper with a pencil.

Next, add a little more modeling clay to raise the end of the marble slide higher. Guess where the marble will hit the floor now. Mark the spot on the paper where you think it will land. Gravity will still pull the marble downward, the same as before, but this time the marble will be traveling faster when it rolls off the end of the table. Do you think the marble will move farther away from the table before gravity causes it to hit the paper?

Try raising and lowering the higher end of the paper towel slide. You and your friends can guess where the marble will land each time. Whoever is closest is the winner.

Does the distance get bigger as the marble slide gets higher?

Project 71
SKI JUMP
Universal pull of gravity

The pull of the Earth's gravity is the same for everything on its surface. But what if you were to *drop* a marble, and at the same time *throw* a second marble from the same height? Would that make a difference, or would both marbles hit the floor at the same time?

You know, of course, that the thrown marble would travel farther away from you, and that gravity would still pull it down, just the same as the marble that was dropped. But this project will prove that even though an object is moving fast parallel to the ground (sideways, not up and down), gravity will make it hit the ground at the same time as a marble simply dropped from the same height.

You will need a table on an uncarpeted, bare floor. Place some cardboard on the table, to keep it clean, and put two mounds of modeling clay on the cardboard. Make one mound only about 1 inch (3 cm) high and the other mound about 6 or 7 inches (15 or 18 cm) high. Push two rulers into one end of the short mound, to form a "V" shape (measuring edge inward). This will make a ramp for a marble to run down. Using two more rulers, make another "V" ramp and set it on the higher clay mound. Mold the clay around the rulers to keep them in place.

You now have two marble ramps, one with a low slope and one with a high slope. Place the low end of the ramps about one inch from the edge of the table.

One marble should be moving more slowly, when it falls from the edge of the table, than the other one from the higher ramp. Listen and your ears will tell you if both marbles hit the floor at the same time. If they do, you will hear the sound of them landing together. If you hear two separate sounds, then the marbles didn't hit at the same time.

You need
- modeling clay
- some cardboard
- 4 rulers
- 2 marbles of equal size
- 2 marbles of different size
- table
- a bare floor under the table

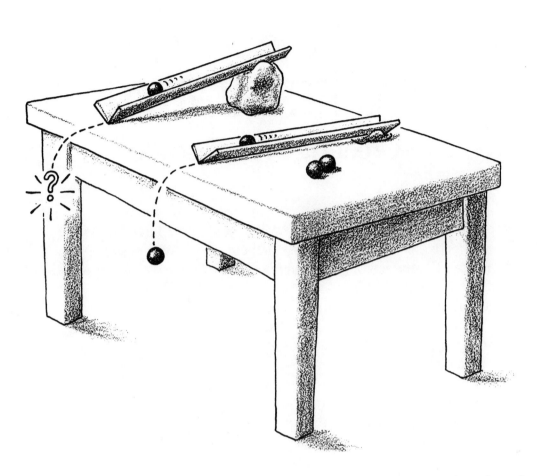

In order for the results to be accurate, both marbles must leave the edge of the table at the exact same time. The marble on the low-sloped ramp will have to start farther up the ramp than the marble on the high-sloped ramp. You will have to experiment letting go of both marbles at different points on the rulers. Use the measurements marked on the rulers as your guides. When you let go of the marbles, listen for the click sound that they make when they hit the tabletop. If you hear more than one sound, then they did not hit the table at the same time, and you will need to change the starting position of one of the marbles.

Once you get both marbles to leave the edge of the table at the same time, listen for the sound of them hitting the floor at the same time. Both marbles will fall the same distance in the same amount of time, but the one moving faster will have traveled farther from the table.

Once you are satisfied with the results of your same-size marble experiments, do the same test using two different-size marbles and compare your results. Does the size of the marbles used count?

Project 72
PAPER MOON
Creating a moonscape

Unlike Earth, the moon has no atmosphere. There's no air or water on the moon, so there's no weather or erosion there. Because of these differences, the surface of the moon does not look like that of the Earth.

Create a model showing the different features of the moon. Some of the features of your moonscape should include seas, craters, rays, rills, domes and scarps.

To make your lunar model, turn a large bowl upside down and cover it with wax paper. Tape the wax paper together and to the bowl to protect it as you form your lunar landscape. The bowl is the mold for the base of your papier-mâché moon.

To make the papier-mâché base, make a sticky paste of flour and water. Mix it until the paste is smooth and easy to work with. Add flour or water if it seems too wet or too dry. Next, tear short strips of newspaper, about 1 inch (3 cm) wide, and dip them in the mixture. Using a crisscross pattern, place the

You need
- 2 large bowls
- wax paper
- adhesive tape
- flour
- water
- strips of newspaper
- modeling clay
- flat stick
- toothpick

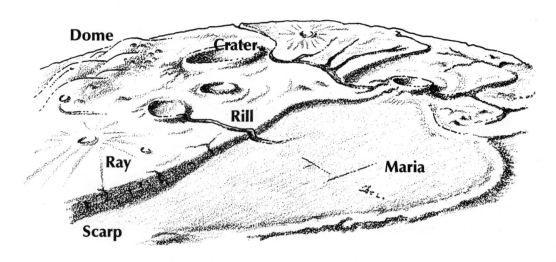

118

coated papier-mâché strips over the whole bowl. Let this covering dry for a few days, then add another layer of papier-mâché and let it dry for several more days.

Instead of using only flour and water, salt can be used in the mixture, or the paper strips can be glued onto the wax-paper-covered bowl to make the base for the lunar landscape.

When dry, cover the whole dome with a layer of modeling clay. Use a flat stick and a toothpick to help you form the different features. Your own Moonscape does not have to be an exact model of Earth's moon. It can just represent the different physical features that are found on the moon.

Lunar Topography

Maria, smooth lunar "seas" that we see from Earth, are large dark plains. Although they are called seas, even on lunar maps, they are not seas at all because there is no water on the moon.

Craters are round low areas surrounded by raised walls, like mountains, forming a circle or ring. Some lunar craters are thousands of miles across and thousands of feet deep.

Rays we see are bright streaks that extend out from the middle of some of the lunar craters. The largest rays can be seen coming from the crater Tycho.

Rills are long narrow trenches. Some are very deep. From Earth they look like winding rivers some hundreds of miles long.

Domes on the moon are smooth, gently sloping, low mounds, like sand dunes, that don't cast any shadows. Most are between 3 and 12 miles (5 and 20 km) across.

Scarps are lunar cliffs. They may be as little as a couple of feet (65 cm) to thousands of feet high.

Project 73
OVER & UNDER
Air movement and air pressure

When you put one end of a straw in your mouth and the other end in a glass of milk or soda can in order to drink, and then suck on it, the liquid travels up the straw. The reason that happens is lower air pressure. How do you know that?

If you put a second straw in your mouth, and don't put the other end into the drink, you will no longer be able to

drink it. You won't be able to lower the air pressure in your mouth by sucking, because air will come in through the second straw. But, pinch the end of the second straw closed, and you are suddenly able to drink the milk or soda again! (Try it and prove it to yourself if you like.)

In addition to helping you use a straw to drink, lower air pressure plays a very important part in keeping airplanes up. How? Let's put on a demonstration.

Push one thumbtack into each side of a wooden doorway, maybe the doorway to your bedroom, at about waist height. Next, tie a string to one thumbtack, stretch the string tightly across the doorway and tie it to the thumbtack on the other side.

You need
- a doorway
- 2 thumbtacks
- string
- long, thin strip of paper
- hair dryer with a cool setting
- stapler or tape

Take a strip of paper about an inch (2.5 cm) wide by 11 or 12 inches (30 cm) long. Fold about a half inch (1 cm) of the end of the paper strip over the string and secure it with a staple or small piece of tape. The loop should be loose enough so the paper moves freely on the string. Gravity will make the paper hang down.

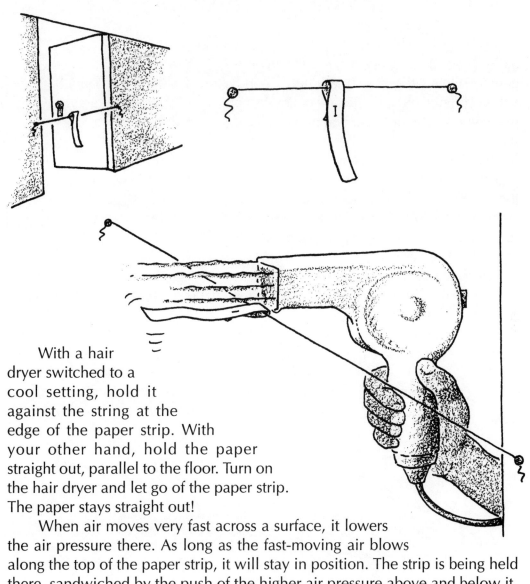

With a hair dryer switched to a cool setting, hold it against the string at the edge of the paper strip. With your other hand, hold the paper straight out, parallel to the floor. Turn on the hair dryer and let go of the paper strip. The paper stays straight out!

When air moves very fast across a surface, it lowers the air pressure there. As long as the fast-moving air blows along the top of the paper strip, it will stay in position. The strip is being held there, sandwiched by the push of the higher air pressure above and below it.

Project 74
DROP ZONE
Parachute design

Sailors have life preservers to use in an emergency; pilots keep their parachutes handy. When you run and fall, the pull of gravity can make you skin your knee. The higher you are when you start falling, like from a chair or ladder, the faster and harder you fall. When a plane is in trouble, using a parachute can save the pilot's life. Parachutes are also used to slow the fall of air-dropped food and supplies to remote places and to bring space capsules safely back to Earth.

> ### You need
> - cloth, two 10-inch (25 cm) squares
> - thread
> - 2 small metal nuts, same size
> - modeling clay
> - scissors (adult help)
> - a height (porch, stairway)

A parachute uses air resistance that stops a falling object from landing so hard. It's called a soft landing. What affects air resistance? Can it be controlled?

The suspension lines tied between the parachute and the harness that a person wears are called shrouds. Is the length of these shroud lines important in the parachute's design? Make two parachutes, having different shroud lengths, and compare their ability to slow an object's fall.

Ask an adult to help you find an old T-shirt, pillow case or bed sheet and cut two 10-inch-square (26-cm) pieces of cloth for the parachutes. (You won't want to cut up good material, and you may need to use extra-sharp scissors to cut the cloth.) Tie four pieces of thread about 6 inches (15 cm)

Cloth

Thread

122

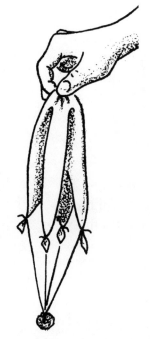

long to a small (¹/₄-inch/¹/₂-cm) nut. Tie one end of each piece of string to a corner of a cloth square.

Tie four pieces of thread 12 inches (30 cm) long to another small nut. Tie one end of each piece of thread to a corner of a cloth square.

Stand where you can drop the parachutes from a height, such as off the side of a porch or flight of stairs.

With one in each hand, hold the two parachutes by pinching the center of the cloths, letting the nuts hang down underneath. Stretch your arms out and let go of both parachutes at the same time.

Do they land on the ground at the same time? If not, which one stays in the air the longest, the one with the 4-inch (10- cm) shroud lines or the one with the 10-inch (26-cm) lines?

Project 75
COOL AIR LIFT
What keeps airplanes up?

Why are airplane wings shaped the way they are? The curve of the wing top forces the air moving over it to travel farther then the air passing underneath, so the air has to move faster. When that happens, it lowers the air pressure above the wing and gives the plane what is known as lift.

You need
- paper towel tube
- pencil with flat sides
- ruler
- hair dryer
- table
- scissors
- 2 books of equal thickness

Ask an adult to cut a paper-towel tube in half, then lengthwise, to make two short curved pieces. Push down a little along one side of the length of one tube to flatten it slightly and give it an airplane-wing shape. One side of the tubing will have more curve: this will be the front. The flatter side, with less curve, will be the back.

Lay two books of the same thickness near the edge of a table. Place them about three inches (7 to 8 cm) apart and lay a pencil across them, from one to the other. Use a pencil with flat sides to keep it from rolling. Put the paper-towel tube wing on the side of a ruler, lined up with the end. Place the ruler and wing on the pencil so that it balances like a seesaw. The end of the ruler with the wing on it should hang out over the edge of the table.

Using a hair dryer on a cool setting, blow air at the curved, front edge of the wing. The air pressure will be lower above the wing as the fast-moving air travels up and around it, and the seesaw balance will begin to tip. Which end rises?

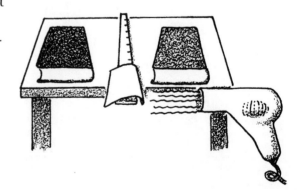

Project 76
MOVE OVER!

Motion beats the power of gravity

You can throw a ball straight up—but not very far. Gravity pulls it down. But your throwing motion does overcome gravity for a short while.

It is possible, however, for motion to overcome gravity. Tie three of the small ($1/4$-inch/ $1/2$-cm) nuts onto the end of a two-foot long (60-cm) piece of string. Pass the other end of the string through the hole of an empty thread spool. Tie one small nut onto that other end of the string. For safety's sake, cover the nuts with some cotton and secure with tape.

You need
- empty thread spool
- some string
- 4 small metal nuts
- cotton
- adhesive tape
- scissors

Hold the spool so that the string is hanging, with the three nuts at the bottom. Gravity is, of course, pulling the three nuts down. Pull several inches of string up out of the top of the spool.

Now, slowly move the spool in a circular motion to swing the upper nut around. The faster you move the spool, swinging the upper nut, the higher the string will come out of the spool, lifting the three nuts on the other end. Be careful as the string is drawn up, making larger and larger circles, so that you are not hit by the swinging nut. It is the action of centrifugal force that is pulling the revolving nut away from the center of the spool and overcoming gravity's pull on the other three nuts.

Project 77
STELLAR PERFORMANCE
The night sky as the Earth turns

As the Earth turns, the stars in the sky above seem to be moving. How fast? Let's track it.

Place a piece of thread straight across the middle of one end opening of a paper-towel tube and tape it in place. Now tape another piece of thread across the opening, but at a 90-degree angle so that the threads cross in the center. The "X" will help you position a star in your viewfinder.

On a clear night, go outside and pick a bright star. Place the view-finder on a support and point it at the star. The end with the thread cross-hairs should be towards the star. Position your viewfinder so that the star you picked appears in the exact center of the tube, right where the two threads cross. Use modeling clay to fix the viewfinder in position. Look at a clock and write down the time.

Once every minute, look through your viewfinder and see if the star has moved. On your paper, draw what you see in the viewfinder and note the time. How long does it take for you to notice that the star is no longer positioned at the X point? How long before the star is completely out of sight in the viewfinder? Now pick a different star and repeat the experiment. Did it take the same amount of time for this star to travel out of sight in your viewfinder?

Project 78
SUN DAY NEWS
The changing length of day and night

Because the Earth turns completely around every twenty-four hours, the sun seems to rise and set once each day. The time between sunrise and sunset is called length of day. Does it change from day to day and month to month? How about the moon? Does the time between moonrise and moonset change each day? How does it compare to the time of sunrise and sunset?

You need
- daily newspaper for 7 days
- paper
- pencil

Buy a newspaper that lists the times of sunrise and sunset, and moonrise and moon-set, each day. Get the paper every day for seven days in a row. Make up a chart showing the time of sunrise and sunset for each day. Calculate the length of day and fill in your chart with the times. Study your chart. Is the length of day getting longer or shorter?

As the Earth travels around the sun, there are two times during the year when day and night are equal in length around the world. This time is called equinox. The vernal (spring) equinox happens around March 20. The autumnal equinox happens around September 22. On the equinoxes, the length of day and night are each twelve hours long, since there are 24 hours in a day.

During the year, there's a time when the length of day is longest, and a time exactly opposite when the length of day is the shortest. The shortest day is called the winter solstice. The longest day is called the summer solstice. In the Northern Hemisphere, the winter solstice happens around December 21. It is officially the first day of winter. The summer solstice happens around June 20, the first day of summer. Look at your chart. Is the length of day getting longer or shorter? According to your chart, are you heading towards the winter solstice or the summer solstice?

Project 79
TWO BRIGHT
Light pollution

Most of us have heard about air pollution, but astronomers and others who enjoy studying the night sky are also aware of light pollution. Light pollution is when the light from homes and businesses, signs, street lamps, neon lights, and other artificial sources "wash out" the dark sky, preventing us from seeing the fainter stars.

Show how bright light can actually keep you from seeing details by washing out your vision.

On a piece of white poster board, clearly write a number of letters of the alphabet, like an eye doctor's testing chart with big letters at the top, a line of smaller letters underneath, and even smaller letters in each line farther down. Start with letters big enough to see from about 20 feet (8 m) away.

On a dark night, have an adult stand in front of an automobile, hold up the poster board, and shine a flashlight on it. Stand facing the automobile, but about 20 feet (8 m) away, and read as many letters as you can.

Next, have the adult turn on the headlights of the automobile behind the poster board. Even though the flashlight is still trained on it, how many letters can you read now, with the headlights on?

Project 80
TOMORROW'S ASTRONAUTS
Visit to a pretend planet

Choose a planet other than the Earth. In order from our sun, they are Mercury and Venus, closer to the sun, and Mars, Jupiter, Saturn, Uranus, Neptune and Pluto, farther away than we are. Go to the library, use your own encyclopedia and reference books, or search the Internet. Learn as much as you can about the planet you choose. Write down where you got each of your facts.

You need
- one or more friends
- arts and crafts supplies
- library research materials
- pencil and paper

Write a script for a skit about what it would be like to travel in a spaceship and land on that planet. Hypothesize what you and your crew would see and feel, based on what you learned in your research. Would you have trouble breathing? Finding food and water? Staying warm? Moving around? How many moons do you see in the sky? How big are they and how do they move? What does the landscape around you look like? What does the Earth look like to you when you are standing on your planet's surface? Can you see the Earth at all? Does your planet revolve? How long are the days and nights there? Is there anything of value on the planet, such as ore that could be mined?

With some friends, or at school, use cardboard and other arts-and-crafts materials to make a ship, scenery and props for your skit. Make spacesuits and other costumes (the planet's native life forms?) for the actors to wear. If you have and can use a video camera, it might be nice to record the skit for a science fair presentation.

Project 81
SUN TREK
Tracking the sun's movement

Every day, as the Earth turns on its axis, the sun seems to move across the sky. To safely track this movement over several hours (never look directly at the sun or you can damage your eyes), we will construct and use a special charting box.

Remove the top flaps from a cardboard box about 2 feet (60 cm) square. Set the box on its side with the opening facing you. Ask an adult to help cut a small hole, a few inches wide, in the top side of the box, near the middle. Place a piece of thin poster board over the hole, closing it up, and tape it in place. Very carefully, make a sharp, tiny hole in the center of the poster board with a safety pin or needle, so that it also passes through the hole in the side of the box.

Inside the box, lay a sheet of white paper on the bottom and tape it down. Take the box outside on a sunny day. Point the top of the box towards the sun. Use a brick or flat board to tilt the box, if the sun is not directly overhead. A small white dot of sunlight will shine through the pinhole onto the paper. With a pencil, mark the spot on the paper where the light hits. Look at a clock and write the time next to the spot. Every half hour, mark the spot where the sunlight hits and write down the time. After several hours, remove the paper and study your marks. It may seem that the marks were tracking the sun, but since the sun does not move, it is actually the Earth's movement that was tracked.

> ### You need
> - cardboard box
> - thin poster board
> - adhesive tape
> - safety pin
> - brick
> - a sunny day
> - scissors
> - unlined white paper
> - clock
> - pencil
> - adult with penknife

Project 82
I AM A SUNDIAL
Telling time from the sun

On a sunny day, unless the sun is directly over your head, your body casts a shadow. Sometimes your shadow is short and sometimes it's long. Did you know that that fact can tell you the time? Take poster boards and tape them end to end to make a large sheet about 3 by 8 feet (100 x 250 cm).

At 1 p.m. on a sunny afternoon, stand outside with your back to the sun. Lay the poster board sheet down on the ground. Stand with the toes of your shoes just touching one edge, so you cast a shadow onto the boards. Have a friend draw the outline of your shadow with a dark crayon or marker. Write the time next to the outline.

> **You need**
> - a sunny afternoon
> - several large poster boards
> - dark marker or crayon
> - clock
> - adhesive tape
> - a friend

At 2 o'clock, in the same place, have your friend draw your shadow again. Write "2 p.m." by the outline. At 3, 4 and 5 o'clock, have your shadow drawn again, marking the time of day. Did your shadow grow longer as the time passed? That means your shadow gets longer as the Earth turns away from the sun.

The next afternoon, take your poster-board "shadow map" outside and stand with your back to the sun. With the map on the ground at your feet and your feet against the boards as before, look at the shadow you cast. Without a clock, about what time is it? You can tell by comparing your shadow now to your outlines from the day before. What do you suppose happens to your shadow in the morning?

Get information on sundials and how they work, then bring your human sundial shadow-map project to school to share with your class.

Project 83
SUNNY SPOTLIGHT
The art of spreading light

Although it may seem that way, it isn't hotter in the summer because the Earth is closer to the sun, and colder in the winter because it is farther away. The seasonal changes from winter, to spring, to summer, to autumn are caused by the Earth's movement around the sun and the fact that the Earth is tilted about 23 degrees, instead of straight up and down like a top. This changes the angle at which sunlight hits the surface of the Earth, as it makes its one-year journey around the sun. The Northern Hemisphere gets more sunlight when the Earth is tipped towards the sun, so it is hotter (summer in the Northern Hemisphere). At the same time, the Southern Hemisphere is

You need
- clipboard
- sheet of unlined paper
- flashlight
- hardback book
- pencil

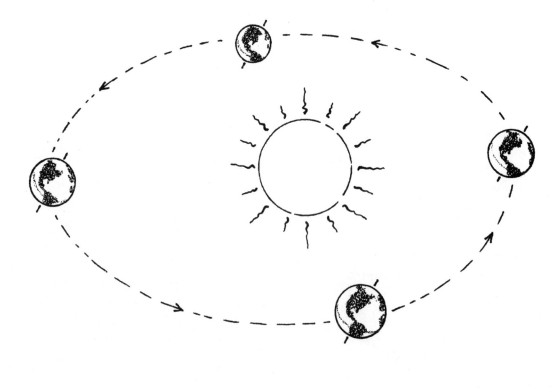

tilted at an angle away from the sun. The sunlight spreads out more thinly over a greater area there, so it is colder (winter in the Southern Hemisphere).

Light rays are strongest when they hit straight on. It is usually hotter at noon, when the sun is right overhead, than in the early morning or late evening. Light is weakest when rays hit a surface on an angle, because the light is forced to spread out and cover more of the surface. Show how light spreads out when it hits a surface tilted at an angle to the light source.

Place a hardback book on a table and open it slightly so it will stand up. Turn a flashlight on and set it on top of the book.

Clip a sheet of unlined white paper onto a clipboard. Hold the clipboard straight up and down in front of the flashlight. With a pencil, draw an outline around the circle of light on the paper.

Now tilt the clipboard away from the flashlight. Draw an outline around the oval of light on the paper.

Compare the circle and the oval. Did the light spread out more when the clipboard was tilted away from the light source?

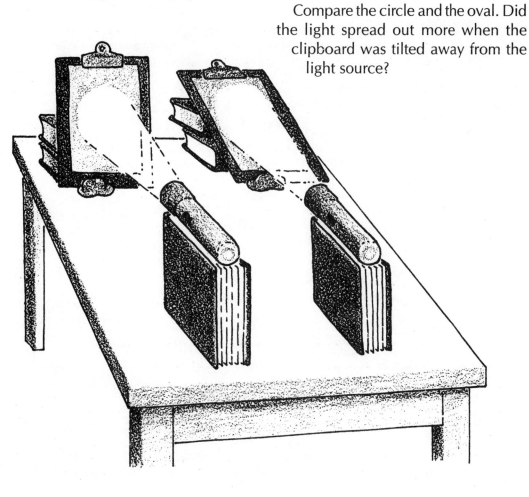

133

Project 84
ONCE AROUND THE SUN
Comparing planetary years

How long is a year? That depends on which planet you are on. The time it takes for the Earth to make one orbit around the sun is one Earth year. The orbits of the different planets are larger the farther away they are from the sun, so it takes them a longer time to go once around the sun. Mercury and Venus are closer to the sun than the Earth is, so a year on those planets is shorter than one Earth year.

You need
- 9 different colors of yarn
- scissors
- masking tape
- a long wall
- research books
- paper and pencil

Research how long it takes each of the nine planets in our solar system to go once around the sun. Find the length of each planet's year in Earth time; for example, it takes Mercury only about 88

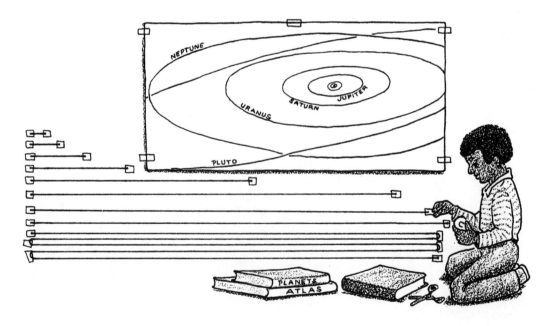

134

Earth days to complete its circle around the sun, while Pluto takes about 247½ Earth years! When you've finished, change the time to months. Mercury, then, would take 3 months, Earth would take 12 months and Pluto 2,970 months.

Gather nine different colors of yarn. Choose a color for each planet. The yarn will represent the length of time it takes for that planet to go around the sun once. One inch, or one centimeter, can represent one month. By that measurement, the length of yarn for Mercury's orbit will be 3 inches or centimeters, Earth's will be 12 and Pluto's will be 2,970!

Near a corner of a long wall, tape one end of each piece of yarn. Keep the yarn pieces separate and straight, and tape up the other ends. Some pieces of yarn, especially the one representing Pluto's year, will be so long you will have to fold them back and forth *several times* along the wall. (If wall space is limited, use smaller measurements. For example, let the length of Mercury's year, 3 months, equal ½ inch, ½ centimeter, etc.)

Label each yarn strand by writing down the name of the planet and the length of its year in Earth time. Adding each planet's symbol (the drawings that represent them) and other information you learn about the planets in our Solar System will make your project even better.

Planets + Symbols

o Mercury ☿

O Venus ♀

O Earth ⊕

o Mars ♂

Jupiter ♃

Saturn ♄

o Pluto ♇ Neptune ♆ Uranus ♅

135

Project 85
JUST ADD AIR
Making environmental changes

There are aircraft known as heavier-than-air (airplanes, helicopters, gliders) and those that are lighter than air (balloons, blimps). Balloons that carry people, weather instruments or other loads rise because the total weight of the gas in the balloon, the balloon itself, the passengers and the basket is still less than the weight of the air that would take up the same amount of space.

We live at the bottom of an ocean of air. Air and water behave much the same way. We can demonstrate the lighter-than-air idea

You need
- an adult with a drill
- plastic soda bottle with screw cap
- water-filled tub or large pail
- small pebbles or stones
- 3 feet (90 cm) of plastic aquarium tubing
- rubber band

by using a bottle in a bathtub full of water.

Have an adult drill three small holes, each about 1/4 inch (7 mm) in diameter, into an empty, plastic soda bottle (16/20 ounce or half liter). The drilled holes need to be about two inches (5 cm) or so up from the bottom of the bottle.

Fill a tub or pail with water. Push the bottle into the water so that the water level is just above the three holes, letting water go into the bottle.

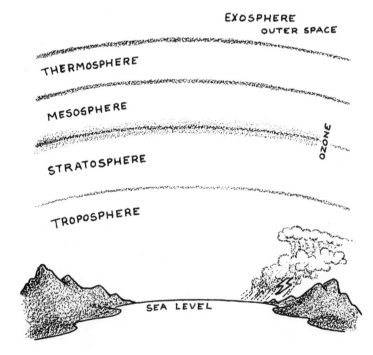

EXOSPHERE
OUTER SPACE

THERMOSPHERE

MESOSPHERE

STRATOSPHERE

OZONE

TROPOSPHERE

SEA LEVEL

The bottle will float.

Drop a few small pebbles into the bottom of the plastic soda bottle. Add pebbles until the bottle sinks. Screw the cap on the bottle.

Take one end of the piece of plastic tubing and stick it into the bottle through one of the small holes. Bending the end upward, push it towards the inside top of the bottle. Place a rubber band around the bottle to hold the tube in place. Next, blow into the tube.

When you blow through the tube and into the bottle, the air pushes water out of the holes and replaces it. The air inside the bottle weighs less than the atmosphere outside the bottle (water), so the bottle rises. You can make the bottle rise and fall in the water by blowing air in or letting air out of the bottle.

Project 86
DRAG ON

Air's resistance to motion

"Drag" is a word used by people in aviation. It means the resistance of air to the forward motion of an aircraft. As an object tries to move faster through the air, the air tries to slow it down.

You need
- 3 sheets of typing paper

Take three sheets of regular typing paper. Hold your hand out at arm's length, with your palm upward. Lay a piece of paper flat on your hand. Pull your hand away. Watch how slowly the paper falls to the floor.

Lightly crumple another piece of paper into a ball. Hold it out at arm's length and drop it. Did the ball of paper push through the air and fall faster?

Make a paper airplane. Hold it out with its nose pointing towards the floor. Let it go.

Which of the three sheets of paper fell the fastest (had the least drag slowing it down)?

Look at the designs of different cars and airplanes. How do their shapes reduce drag and allow them to move faster through the air? How can you use that information the next time you take part in a race?

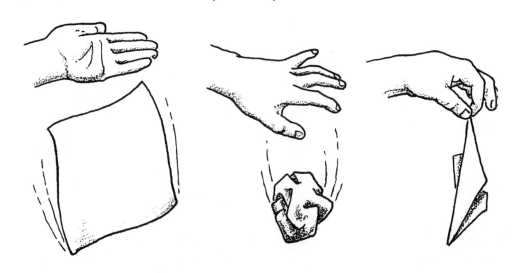

Project 87
NO STRINGS
Balancing with pressures

It might look like magic to suspend a Ping-Pong ball in midair, without anything touching it, but it's not. The secret is balancing air push and pressure, and, voilà! The ball floats!

Place a hair dryer on a table and point it so the flow of air will go straight up. Several hardbound books will hold the dryer in place. Set the hair dryer to the fastest speed but the coolest position and turn it on. Gently place a Ping-Pong ball in the middle of the air column from the dryer. Let go of the ball, and it will stay in place, hovering over the hair dryer as if by magic.

> **You need**
> - hair dryer
> - several hardbound books
> - Ping-Pong ball
> - stiff cardboard about 5 or 6 inches (12 or 15 cm) square
> - table

Now, take a piece of stiff cardboard or poster board. Holding the stiff board upright, slowly move it towards the floating ball. As the board nears the ball, the ball will start to move towards the cardboard. In order to squeeze between the board and ball, the moving air is forced to speed up. When the air moves faster, it causes a drop in air pressure, so the ball is pushed by higher air pressure in that direction. This is what happens to airplanes in flight. Pilots have to be ready to adjust for air pressure differences caused by weather or, if they are flying low, by differences in the landscape.

Can you make the ball go higher by making the air from the dryer move even faster? Try covering part, half or more of the hair dryer opening with a piece of cardboard and see what happens.

Project 88
WANE, WANE, GO AWAY
Charting the phases of the moon

As the nights go by, the moon seems to change shape. At times, only a thin curved piece, a "crescent," is visible. It appears to grow bigger each day until it becomes a round, brightly lit disc. Then it starts to disappear, with less and less of the moon being seen. Finally, it is only a crescent again, and then the moon vanishes altogether.

These changes in the appearance of the moon are called "phases." It takes a little over 28 days for the moon to go through its pattern of changes and start over again. The moon, of course, doesn't really change shape. It is always round. It's the light from the sun, shining on the moon, that causes the changes we see. It is true that the sun is always shining on the moon, but we here on

You need
- one month
- paper and pencil

The Lunar Phases

Astronomers have named several stages of the moon's phases. A "New Moon" is when you can't see it at all. A "Full Moon" is a completely lit moon. If you take the new, full, and two phases in between (which make four phases), you can call a halfway lit moon the "first quarter" and "last quarter" phases. In between those times are "crescent" phases, when only a small curved piece is lit, and "gibbous" phases, when *all but* a small curved piece is lit and the moon looks like a football.

When the crescent and gibbous phases are working towards a Full Moon stage, they are said to be "waxing," or building up. When the crescent and gibbous phases are heading towards a New Moon, it is called "waning." (A wane, wane moon soon "goes away.")

Earth can only see the lit side that's facing us. We can't see the dark side against the dark sky.

Every evening for a month, look at the moon and draw what you see. Don't worry about skipping a night if you can't watch, or when the sky is overcast or it is raining. The changes in the moon's phases happen slowly, and you won't miss much by not watching one night.

When you have completed your moon chart for a month, you can use it as a guide. Then, when you look at the moon, you will be able to tell which part of the cycle it is in, and predict if it is heading towards a "Full Moon" or a "New Moon."

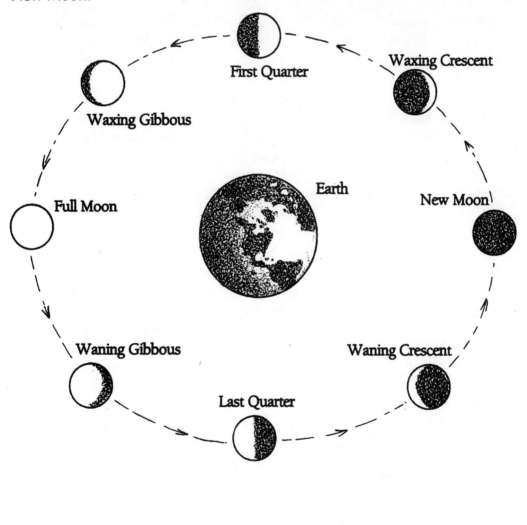

Project 89
TILT!

Our solar system's leaning planets

The sun's planets orbit it, moving roughly along the same flat plane, except for Pluto which orbits slightly above it. This plane is an imaginary line that can be drawn through two points on the Earth's orbit; this so-called orbital plane extends across and out past all the planets. Think of the sun as being in the middle of a gigantic plate, and all the planets placed on the flat plate, or plane, around it.

You need
- 9 pencils
- modeling clay
- toothpicks
- paper or index cards
- protractor
- research books
- adhesive tape
- hardbound book

If you were to also draw an imaginary line through the North and South Poles of a planet (the axis on which a planet turns), you would find that some planets are tilted. The axis isn't perpendicular (90 degrees) to the plane of the orbit. In other words, the planets are not spinning straight up; they are not as a book standing up on a table is perpendicular to it.

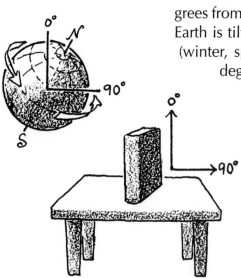

The Earth, for example, is tilted at about 23 degrees from the perpendicular to its orbit. Because the Earth is tilted, we have the changing of the seasons (winter, spring, summer and fall). Pluto has a 17-degree tilt. Uranus is really weird, spinning on its side at a 98-degree angle!

Make nine balls out of modeling clay, one for each planet in our solar system. You may make some balls bigger than the others, since the planets are different sizes, but the balls don't have to be made to scale. Push a pencil through the middle of each ball. This will represent the planet's axis, the imaginary line around which the planet spins.

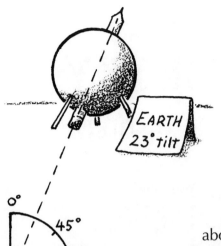

Write the name of each planet on small pieces of paper or cards that you can bend and stand in front of each clay model. Research the angle of tilt for each planet and put that information on the cards.

Using adhesive tape, stick a protractor onto the side of a tabletop, so that the 90 degree mark is in line with the table's surface (see illustration) and the 0 degree mark is straight up. Set a clay ball next to the protractor. Turn the ball so that the pencil is at about the angle the planet is tilted. Push three toothpicks into the bottom of the ball, making a set of three (tripod) legs for it to stand on. Do this for each of the nine planets.

When you set the model planets on a table, put Pluto up on a book to raise it. above the plane of the surface. This will represent the number of degrees that Pluto is above the plane of the solar system.

Project 90
RINGS IN THE SKY
A motion study of Saturn's rings

A number of planets have rings encircling them, but the most spectacular by far are those around Saturn. It's thought that Saturn's rings are made up of an almost infinite number of ice crystals and ice-covered particles. Some of the particles are as small as a grain of sand and others are as big as a house.

Saturn is tilted on its axis (see Project 89) about 28 degrees and takes almost 30 Earth years (see Project 84) to complete one orbit around the sun. As the Earth and Saturn orbit the sun, we are able to see Saturn from different angles. Sometimes, when the rings are edge on, we can only see a thin line extending out from both sides of the planet. At other times, we can see the rings more fully. Imagine bending down and looking at your kitchen table edge on. You can't see the top of the table, only the edge. Then stand up. Now you can see the whole top, and how long and wide the table really is.

You need
- softball
- adhesive tape
- crayons or markers
- stiff paper or poster board
- modeling clay
- a large room
- basketball
- ball of string
- small cardboard box
- paper-towel tube
- magnetic compass
- 5 chairs
- clock
- a friend
- dominos or markers
- protractor

Two views of Saturn's rings

To demonstrate what can see of Saturn and its rings from Earth, try this project.

Use a softball, or similar-size ball, to represent Saturn. From stiff paper or poster board, cut a wide ring to fit around the ball. Color the ring, making bright, different colored circles going around it. Add some small dots to represent larger orbiting rocks. Tape the ring into position on the softball. Use modeling clay to form a base to hold your "softball Saturn." Using a protractor, tilt Saturn at the correct 28-degree angle for the planet.

Outside or in a large open room, place a basketball, to represent the sun, in the center. Taking some string about 31fi feet long (10fi m) and another 63 feet long (21 m), tie the ends together to make two string circles. Spread the two string circles out around the basketball. The larger circle, about 20 feet (6 m) in diameter, represents Saturn's orbit around the sun. The smaller inner circle, about 10 feet (3 m) in diameter, represents the Earth's orbit around the sun.

Now, replace the basketball, for the moment, with a clock lying on its back and facing up. Using dominos, or other such items, mark off twelve spots along the string of Saturn's orbit. To position the markers, attach a length of string to the center of the cloth and use the numbered hours as your guide. Pass a length of string straight across the face of the clock. If a friend is available to help, you each can mark off six positions by passing the string directly across the center of the cloth.

Along the inner string, representing Earth's orbit, place four chairs: one at the 12 o'clock, 3 o'clock, 6 o'clock and 9 o'clock positions. This represents the four positions, or seasons, of Earth's year.

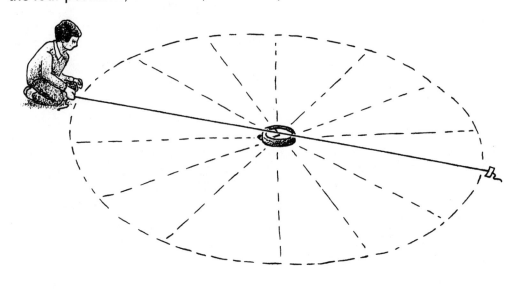

Place a chair at the 12 o'clock position on Saturn's orbit. Put a small cardboard box on the chair and place your Saturn on it. Sit in the chair at the 12 o'clock position on Earth's orbit and look at Saturn. It should be at eye level. If it is too high, use a smaller cardboard box.

Using adhesive tape, mount a magnetic compass to the top of the cardboard box under the "softball Saturn." Where the needle points to North, draw a line on the box with a crayon or marker. During the experiment, you will be moving the Saturn chair around the room in a circle. Each time you move the chair, be sure the the compass needle lines up with the mark on the box.

With Saturn at the 12 o'clock position, sit in each of the four chairs on Earth's orbit. Pretend the empty paper-towel tube is a telescope and look through it. This is how Saturn will look from Earth for 2½ years.

Now move Saturn to the 1 o'clock position, and again sit in each of the four chairs on Earth's orbit. Each of the 12 locations for Saturn represents about 2½ years of the planet's position. Continue to do this for all 12 Saturn positions and you will see how Saturn will look from Earth for thirty years, when the cycle begins again. Did you notice the differences in the ring positions at the different times?

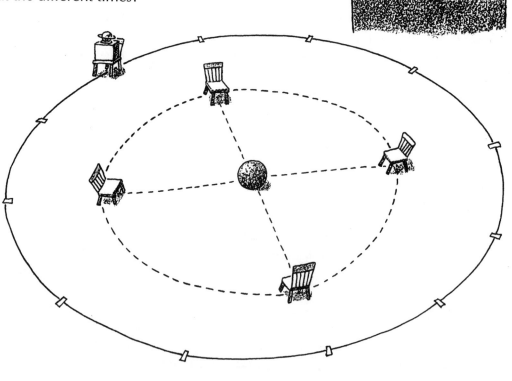

Project 91
BIG EYE IN THE SKY
Tasks for a special telescope

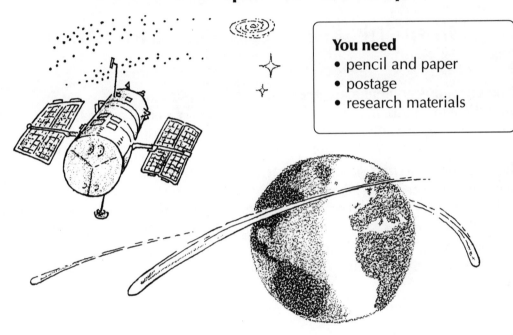

You need
- pencil and paper
- postage
- research materials

In 1990, the Space Shuttle launched the Hubble Space Telescope. This telescope orbits the Earth and provides astronomers with a new tool to use in their work. Named after Edwin Hubble, a famous American astronomer, the Hubble Space Telescope can see things too faint to be detected with telescopes on Earth. Also, because the telescope is above Earth's atmosphere, it has a much clearer view of what it sees. Objects are not distorted by the shifting gases, moisture and particles that make up the Earth's atmosphere. What does this mean? Many stars twinkle when we view them from Earth. Do they twinkle when seen by the Hubble?

Scientists propose ideas to the National Aeronautics and Space Administration (NASA) for using the Hubble Space Telescope. Your challenge is to read all you can about this great research tool and learn what it is capable of doing. Then design a job for the Hubble to do.

Write to NASA and suggest your experiment to them. What is their response?

Project 92
SOUTH OF THE BORDER
Different skies for North and South

The equator is an imaginary line around the middle of the Earth. It is located midway between the North and South Poles. The equator divides the Earth into two parts called hemispheres, or *half* spheres. Because the Earth is tilted on its axis, the Northern Hemisphere experiences summer when the Southern Hemisphere is having winter. Also, those living in each hemisphere see a different part of the sky. The most famous star pattern seen in the Southern Hemisphere is the Southern Cross—in the Northern Hemisphere it is the Big Dipper.

You need
- pencil and paper
- postage
- research materials

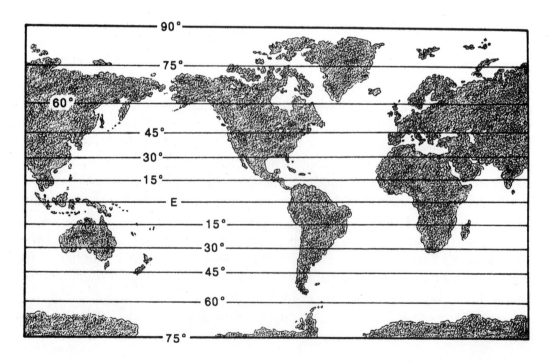

Maps and globes often have grid lines drawn on them, called lines of latitude and longitude. These imaginary lines are used to find the location of any place on Earth. The lines measure degrees on the Earth's surface. There are 89 equally spaced lines of latitude in the Northern Hemisphere, between the equator (0 degrees) and the North Pole (90 degrees north), and 89 more in the Southern Hemisphere, between the equator (0 degrees) and the South Pole (90 degrees south).

Using an atlas or other reference book, find out the latitude where you live. Find another city or town that lies on the same latitude as your town, but in the opposite hemisphere. If you are at 77 degrees *north,* look for a town at 77 degrees *south.* Write a letter to the board of education in the town you have selected, and tell them you would like a pen pal to write to in their school to discuss astronomy. Try to select a place where they speak the same language as you do, unless you would like a pen pal to help you learn another language or to practice a second language on.

Once you have a pen pal, share with your pal what you each see in your evening sky. Draw and exchange the popular star patterns seen in the sky, giving the names of the bigger stars and other interesting information.

Project 93
IS IT NIGHT YET?

How long is twilight?

After the sun sets, it continues to light the Earth's atmosphere for some time. This time, between daylight and dark, is called the twilight hour, or dusk. How long does it take, after sunset, to really get dark?

On a clear evening when there's no moon in the sky, find a place nearby that is away from street or house lights. If you are in your yard, turn off any lights around your house that would keep your area from being

You need
- a clear, dark evening
- clock
- a book
- solar calculator
- an area away from lights
- daily newspapers

really dark. Find out from your daily newspaper or an almanac what time sunset will be that evening. Just before that time, try reading a paragraph from a book and from a newspaper. Add some numbers on a solar calculator.

After the sun has set, try reading another paragraph in your book and

one from the newspaper. Add some more numbers on the calculator. Do these things again every ten minutes.

How long after sunset does the solar calculator stop working? How long until you can no longer read from the book, from the newspaper? (Newspaper type is often smaller and harder to read than type in a book.)

Think of some other ways that you can measure how dark it is at a given time after sunset.

Project 94
SEEING RED, BLUE, &...
Determining colors in dimming light

As the sun goes down and darkness comes, it becomes harder to see. Is it more difficult to see colors after the sun sets? If so, which colors are the hardest to identify when the light gets dim?

Draw two crossed lines on a paper plate, dividing it into four equal parts. With a red crayon or marker, color two opposite sections of the plate, and leave the other two parts white. Do the same with four other plates, using a different color—blue, orange, yellow or green—on two of the sections.

Attach a handle to each plate. You can use a ruler, tongue depressor (available at any pharmacy) or some other long and narrow wooden strip or stick. Tape your strips to the plates, leaving enough "handle" to make it easy for someone to hold the plates up.

When the sun is setting, find a safe area nearby away from bright lights. Have a friend take ten paces from you, then hold up one plate at a time, asking you the color on each plate. Then have your friend take ten more steps away from you and quiz you on the colors again. Your friend should mix up the colored plates, so they are not in the same order each time. Again, have your friend take another ten steps away from you, for a distance of 30 paces away. Can you correctly guess all the colors? Have your friend quiz you on the colors while standing at 10 paces, 20 paces and 30 paces every ten minutes. Do this for one hour. What colors are the hardest to see? How long after sunset are you able to recognize each color?

You need
- crayons or colored markers
- 5 paper plates
- 5 flat sticks (rulers, tongue depressors)
- a cloudless, dark evening
- a friend
- adhesive tape

Project 95
COLOR ME WARM
The effect of sunlight on colored objects

In a town in our area, the city officials thought it would be a good idea to build an ice-skating rink for the community. They formed a big rink out of asphalt and filled it with water. It got cold that winter, well below the freezing point many times. But the kids were disappointed because the water in the ice skating rink never froze! Why? It has to do with the color of asphalt—black.

The sun warms our planet. Things that are dark in color hold sunlight, and the sun's energy warms them. Things that are light in color reflect more sunlight, so are not warmed as much. What colors hold the heat from sunlight the best?

You need
- 4 empty 2-liter plastic bottles
- a 2-liter bottle of cola
- 5 thermometers
- string
- 5 sticks
- table
- sunny window
- red, blue, and yellow food coloring
- pencil and paper
- clock

152

Fill four 2-liter plastic soda bottles with water. In one, add red food coloring. In another, add blue food coloring. Add yellow to another. Be sure the colors are strong and deep. Leave one bottle with just clear water. To test the color black, use a 2-liter bottle of cola soda.

Place all five bottles in a sunny window. Leave them there for about an hour.

In the meantime, cut some strings about 5 inches (13 cm) long Tie one end of each string onto each thermometer and the other end to a small stick or piece of wood. The string should be long enough so that, when the thermometer is lowered into the bottle and the stick rests on top, the bulb of the thermometer will be about halfway down the bottle.

After the hour has passed, check that the thermometers all read about the same temperature. If one or two are reading higher than the others, shake them to get the temperature down. Then lower all five thermometers in the bottles, one in each, and wait five minutes. One by one, bring the thermometer up, read the temperature, write it down, and lower it again. Do this twice. If the temperature is the same, write the temperature down. If not, wait a moment and check the thermometer again, until you get the same reading a second time.

Which bottle collected the most heat energy? How can you use this information on which colors hold heat or reflect light?

Project 96
I SEE THE MOON
Comparing views of the moon

Binoculars and telescopes have lenses that let us see distant objects up closer. On an evening when the moon is full, take a pencil and paper, look up, and draw the features and patterns you can see on the surface of the moon using only your eyes.

Then look through a pair of binoculars, opera glasses, or small telescope and draw the patterns you can see using these different optical instruments. You will be able to see more as lens strength increases. Compare the drawings. Make a list of the differences and similarities. Which instrument has the stronger or weaker lenses?

You need
- an evening with a Full Moon
- binoculars, telescope, or other viewing instrument
- pencil and paper

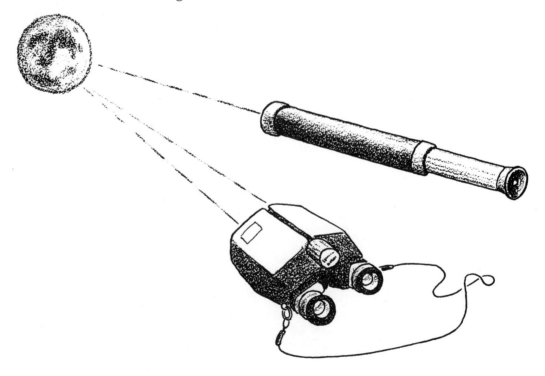

Project 97
PEDAL POWER
How high the moon?

Imagine a spaceship that runs on "pedal power," like a bicycle. Then imagine a road stretching from the Earth to the moon. If you could pedal 10 miles or kilometers per hour without stopping, how long would it take you to reach the moon? If you started now, how old would you be when you got there?

Research the distance in miles/kilometers between the Earth and the moon. Divide that by 10 per hour. The answer will be the number of hours it would take you at that speed.

Convert the number of hours for your trip into days by dividing by 24 hours, because there are 24 hours in a day. How would you convert the hours into weeks? Into years?

Once you know how long the trip would take, add that time to your age today. Exactly how old would you be when you got there if you left today? How old when you got back?

Astronomers have to work with big numbers and long periods of time like this every day, because of the vastness of space. Mathematics is a very important part of astronomy.

You need
- pencil and paper
- research material

Project 98
WORDS CROSSING
Creating science puzzles

Make your own crossword puzzle using words related to flight, space and astronomy. First select a topic, such as "Flight." Then think of a dozen or so words to use in the puzzle; for example, pitch, yaw, roll, plane, flight, lift, balloon, altimeter, climb, propeller, drag, plane, jet, airport. Shaping all those words into a crossword puzzle may seem hard to do, but there is a trick that can make it much easier.

You need
- pencil
- graph paper with large blocks
- scissors

Take a sheet of grid paper with large-sized squares and print the list of words across, one letter to each block. Then print the words a second time, but this time write them reading down instead of across. Take a pair of scissors and cut out each word.

156

Place the longest word (going across) on a clean sheet of grid paper. Lay other words over it, reading down, wherever the letters match. Then continue to lay more words over the other words. Once you use a word, set aside the second copy of that word, because you only want to use each word once in the puzzle. Juggle the words around until you have a nicely shaped crossword puzzle. Leave out words that just won't fit in, and add other words you think of while you're constructing the puzzle that will work okay and fit the topic.

Next, research the meaning of each word and write some clues. In the first block of each word (starting at the top, then right to left), number the word. Match your definitions to the numbers and separate the clues into Across and Down columns.

Color in the empty blocks on the paper, in and around your puzzle, where no letters appear. Lift the beginning of each word carefully, one by one, and write the word number in the blank square under the first letter before you remove the word. Write the number in the upper left-hand corner as small as you can. You need to leave room for the person working the puzzle to fill in the letter.

Science Crosswords

"Planetary Words" might include: Saturn, Mars, Jupiter, Venus, Mercury, orbit, ellipse, ring, rotate, axis.

"Astronomy" might include the words: asteroid, galaxy, comet, nebula, nova, pulsar, planetarium, telescope, astrolabe, meteor, star.

Project 99
SCREENED IMAGES
How the eye sees

Binoculars and telescopes use lenses to magnify images. But the first optical tool ever used in astronomy is actually the human eye. Objects reflect light that enters the eye through the pupil, then passes through a lens that focuses the image onto the area at the back of your eye called the retina (something like film in a camera).

You need
- hand magnifying glass
- modeling clay
- a few small toys
- high-intensity desk lamp
- adhesive tape
- strip of stiff white paper
- table
- scissors
- an adult

Let's set up a demonstration of how the lens works in your eye and in a telescope. Using modeling clay, form a base to hold a small, hand magnifying glass upright and place it on a table. At the other end of the table, place a few small toys (blocks, trucks, dolls) in a group. Have an adult plug in a high-intensity desk lamp and shine the bright light on the toys.

Hold a 3-inch-wide (8-cm) strip of stiff white paper next to the lens of the magnifying glass, on the side opposite the lamp and toys. Slowly move the paper away from the lens until the image of the toys appears in focus. This is the correct imaging distance. Roll the paper strip into an eye-shaped curve. Fix the paper into this correct position by taping the two ends of the paper strip to the magnifying glass lens.

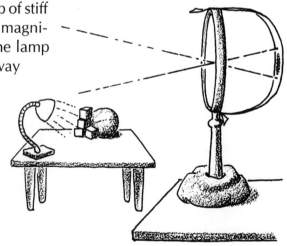

Project 100
FOCUS ON LIGHT BEAMS
Understanding the refracting telescope

A telescope is an instrument that allows distant objects to appear close up. Its name comes from the Greek words *tele,* meaning "from afar," and *skopos,* "viewer." Telescopes gather light and focus it, making objects appear nearer than they really are and letting us see them in more detail. Even the simplest telescope reveals things in the sky that the unaided eye cannot see: the rings of Saturn, craters on the moon, and the bands around Jupiter. In 1608, the Italian scientist Galileo Galilei was the first astronomer to use a telescope. There are different kinds of telescope. One that uses two lenses, instead of one, is called a refracting telescope.

You need
- 2 hand magnifying glasses
- modeling clay
- table near a window
- white paper
- sunny day
- 2 pieces of cardboard

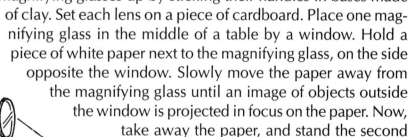

Stand two magnifying glasses up by sticking their handles in bases made of clay. Set each lens on a piece of cardboard. Place one magnifying glass in the middle of a table by a window. Hold a piece of white paper next to the magnifying glass, on the side opposite the window. Slowly move the paper away from the magnifying glass until an image of objects outside the window is projected in focus on the paper. Now, take away the paper, and stand the second magnifying glass at that exact spot. Place your eye next to the second magnifying glass and slowly move away from it until an image of objects outside comes in focus. Do the objects appear bigger? You have made a simple telescope.

The ENVIRONMENT

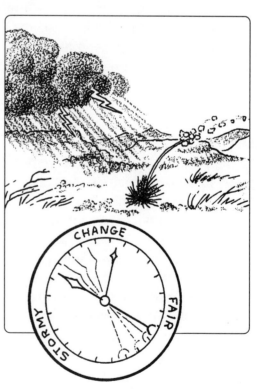

A Note to the Parent

Welcome to the exciting exploration of the world around us...the world of science.

Our environment provides us with many things to observe and processes to understand. Knowledge is gained by observing and questioning.

Science should be enjoyable, interesting, and thought-provoking. That is the concept the writers wish to convey. While this book presents many scientific ideas and learning techniques that are valuable and useful, the approach is designed to entice the young child with the excitement and fun of scientific investigation.

The material is presented in a light and interesting fashion. The concept of measurement can be demonstrated by teaching precise measuring in inches or centimetres, or by having a child stretch his or her arms around a tree trunk and asking, "Are all children's reaches the same?" We present science in such a way, so that it does not seem like science.

The scientific concepts introduced here will help the young student to later understand more advanced scientific principles. Projects will develop those science skills needed in our ever-increasingly complex society: skills such as classifying objects, making measured observations, thinking clearly, and accurately recording data. Values are dealt with in a general way. One should never harm any living thing just for the sake of it. Respect for life should be fundamental. Disruption of natural processes should not occur thoughtlessly and unnecessarily. Interference with ecological systems should always be avoided.

The projects in this book have ben designed as "around you science," in contrast to book science. By "around you science," we mean doing a project right where you are- in your home, your neighborhood, your school. Investigations can even begin at your feet. What is living under that old board lying on the ground? What species of insect are lying now on your windowsill trapped by the screen? How many rings can you count in the trunk of the tree your neighbor has just cut down? Are some rings closer together than others? Why? Since the environment takes in everything around us, the projects in this book cross over into many science disciplines: biology, weather, physics, botany, chemistry, behavior, and even consumerism. Get excited with your child about the world around us!

Project 101
NOWHERE TO BE SEEN
Finding evidence of animal presence

The planet Earth is full of living things. Many times we can tell that an animal has been in a place, even though it is not there now. Hypothesize that you can prove that animals have been in your house, yard, neighborhood, or park. See if you can find proof that ten different animals have been there and gone. Before you start, think about what kind of animals might be around. Make up your "guess list," then start your search for evidence. Make a record of whatever you find.

Some things to look for are: animal hair on the furniture, a smell (a skunk is a good example), a sound (a woodpecker or cricket may be heard but not seen), a mound of sand

You need
- an adult
- outdoor area
- an adult

or a hole in the ground, a chewed leaf, a nest, scratched trees or broken branches, a cocoon or a web, waste products, skeletons or empty shells, holes in trees, tracks on the ground. Look closely. What do you see?

Something more
Can you find evidence of something that animals did? If you find parts of a fly in a spiderweb, even if you don't see the whole fly or the spider, you can guess that there was a struggle between these two animals.

Project 102
FRUIT FOR THOUGHT

Using senses to recognize fruits

We gather information about our environment (the things around us) by using our five senses: seeing, hearing, touching, smelling, and tasting. We use different senses to know about different things. You can't listen to garlic, or smell the sound of music.

To study the senses, let's test the ability of someone to identify fruits by using each sense of the five senses one at a time. Before that person comes, remove a small section of peel from each of four fruit (orange, apple, grapefruit, and banana) and place one in each of the four containers. With a marker, number the lids (not see-through) 1, 2, 3, and 4. Make a list of the numbers and the fruit peel inside each container.

> **You need**
> - 4 small butter or margarine containers with lids
> - 4 fruits: orange, apple, grapefruit, banana
> - a friend or parent
> - paper and pencil

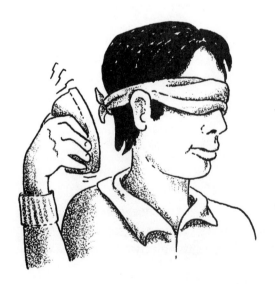

Put the four containers in a row on a table or counter in front of your test subject or friend. Explain that you are conducting a test on fruit identification, then blindfold your friend and start the test. Each time you finish testing one sense below, write down what your friend tells you.

Hearing: Have your friend pick up each container and shake it. Does the sound reveal anything about the fruit peel? What does your friend tell you about each container? Write it down.

Smelling: One at a time, have your friend open a container and smell the contents. Write down what your friend tells you.

Touching: This time, have your friend open each container and reach inside. Can you friend recognize a fruit by feeling the peel? Again, write down what your friend tells you.

Tasting: Now, again one at a time, let your friend taste each peel, or a section of the fruit. What does your friend say now?

Seeing: Take off the blindfold. Let your friend open each container, look inside, and tell you now, if he or she can, which fruits they are. Write it down.

How did your friend do? Do this activity with other friends. How many do you think will be able to guess the fruits? Which senses work best for this activity? Which senses did not help much?

Something more
Use other things in the test. Try smelling different odors, tasting different liquids. Can you feel the difference between coins?

Project 103
THE GREAT SOAP RACE
Comparing how long soaps last

Soap is one of the most common things found in the home. We use soap to clean our houses, hair, cars, dishes, and our bodies. The soaps we use to clean our bodies come in bars of different shapes, smells, and sizes. When we use a bar of soap to wash up, it gets smaller. Which brand of soap lasts the longest?

Go to the store with an adult and help select four different kinds of bar soap. Ask to have a small piece of soap cut from each bar. Each piece should be the same size.

Get four small pieces of paper. On the first piece write #1 and the name of one of the soap brands. On the second piece of paper, write #2 and the name of another soap brand. On the third piece of paper write #3 and the name of the third brand of soap. On the fourth piece of paper write #4 and the name on that bar of soap.

Place the four pieces of paper next to each other on a table. Fill four clear drinking glasses with warm water. Each glass should contain the same amount of water. On each piece of paper, place one glass of warm water and put a piece of the soap brand written on the paper into the water.

After a while, look at the pieces of soap. Which one is the smallest? Which piece is the largest? Look again later. Did the smallest piece dissolve completely? How long did it take for the different brands to dissolve?

Don't waste, recycle. Put the soapy water into a plastic bottle to use as liquid soap.

Something more
Do you think that the soap that lasted the longest would make the most lather? Which brand costs the most? Does the longest-lasting soap also cost the least? Does the soap that lasts the longest also smell the best? If a bar of soap has a nice smell, does it last longer than most other soaps? Do any of the soaps float?

Project 104
PEOPLE MIGRATION
Determining traffic patterns

Some animals migrate. That means they move from one place to another. If you live in a northern climate, there will be some birds that fly south for the winter. They come back in the spring when the weather gets warmer. In mountainous areas, some animals migrate to the valleys in the winter and go back up in the summer. They have trouble finding food in the mountains in the winter snow, so they come down where there isn't as much snow.

You need
- pencil and paper
- a two-way street or road near your home
- an adult, in high traffic areas

How do people move during the day? Do they drive one way in the morning to go to work and then travel the other way to go home? Stand on a sidewalk or roadside near your home and count the number of cars that pass by. Do this for fifteen minutes before you go to school in the morning, and then again for fifteen minutes in the early evening. A friend can help by counting the cars going one way while you count the cars going the other way.

CARS →
15 minutes in
MORNING:
卌 卌 卌 ll

15 minutes in
AFTERNOON:
卌 卌 卌 卌
卌 llll

← CARS
15 minutes in
MORNING:
卌 卌 卌 卌
卌 卌 卌 卌
卌 卌 卌 ll

15 minutes in
AFTERNOON:
卌 卌 lll

To count the cars, draw one line for each car on a piece of paper. Do this for four cars, and then draw a line across the four lines to count the fifth car. This makes groups of five. It is easier to add numbers together if they are grouped. Do you think that many of the people who go by your house in the morning, go back the opposite way at night?Something more

Look at the numbers from the morning and afternoon counts. When were there more cars? If more cars went one way in the morning, did more cars go the other way in the afternoon? If more cars go one way one morning, will this be true every morning? Try counting the passing cars at the same time for five days, beginning Monday and ending Friday. Are there always more cars going one way than the other in the morning?

Many people work Monday through Friday. How do the numbers change if you count on a Saturday or a Sunday?

You may want to try counting at different times of the morning and afternoon. You could count for more than fifteen minutes, perhaps a half hour or an hour.

Is there anything near your home that might affect your count? A cinema, sports arena, shopping mall, or school?

NUMBER OF CARS IN 30 MINUTES

Project 105
ORDER OUT OF CHAOS
How to classify things

One of the skills scientists must have is to be able to classify things. Things can be put into groups, or classifications, when something about them is the same, like color or size.

Gather twenty different stones from around your neighborhood. Put three paper plates on a table. Group the stones by their size. Put small stones on one plate, medium-sized stones on another plate, and the biggest stones on the last plate. Count how many stones you put in each group, and write the number down

Empty the plates and put all the stones back in one pile. Now group them by light and dark color. Put light-colored stones on one plate, dark ones on another plate, and mixed or medium ones on the last. Count how many stones you put in each group and write it down.

Something more

Can you think of other ways to group your stones? Can you group them by heavy and light? Can you group them by smooth and rough?

Find out which stone is the hardest by seeing which one will scratch another. Make a chart showing the characteristics of each stone. Pick up a geology book at your library to identify your stones and find out about them.

Project 106
HOME COMFORTABLE HOME

Temperature in your home environment

There's no place like home ... a place where you feel happy and comfortable. Even though your home has heat in the winter and fans or air-conditioning in the summer, some places in your home may not be as comfortable as others because of the temperature. Some spots may be comfortable at one time of the day, but uncomfortable at another time.

> **You need**
> - thermometer
> - pencil and paper
> - an adult (for safety around heat sources

Measure the temperatures of different areas of your home in the morning, at noon, and in the evening. Which are the most comfortable areas, and at what times of day? Write down the location, the temperature, the time, and whether you are comfortable or uncomfortable there.

Sitting by a window may be comfortable and warm during the day, when the sun is shining in, but cold and uncomfortable in the evening, when a leaky window allows a cold winter draft to blow through.

What is the temperature near your home's source of heat (air ducts, radiators, electric baseboards, fireplace)? Is there a spot near a sunny window that doesn't need any other heat when the sun is shining in?

Something more
In a heated room, do you feel uncomfortable even though the temperature is just right? If your skin feels dry, maybe it's because there is not enough moisture in the air.

171

Project 107
NUKED BEANS
The effect of microwaves on seeds

Microwave ovens use powerful radio (electromagnetic) waves to heat food. These waves can be dangerous to people; that is why the makers of these ovens build them in a way that keeps the microwaves safely inside. They put special switches on the oven doors: the switch turns the power off if anyone opens the door. This keeps the people who use the microwave ovens safe from the invisible waves inside.

What about those unseen radio waves trapped inside the oven? Do you think that

You need
- an adult
- microwave oven
- 12 bean seeds
- potting soil
- plastic or plastic-foam egg carton
- water
- marking pen
- pencil and paper

they could hurt seeds?

Fill an egg carton with potting soil. Use a carton that is made of plastic or plastic foam so that it won't leak when water is poured into it.

Use a marking pen to write the number "0" by the first two pockets, "5" by the second set of pockets, "10" by the third, "15", "20", and "25" by the next ones. These numbers stand for the number of seconds the beans will spend in the microwave.

Put a bean in each of the two pockets by the number "0". The zero means that these seeds spent no time in the oven.

Have an adult put two beans in a microwave oven and turn it on for 5 seconds on a low power setting. Then plant the beans in the egg carton in the pockets marked "5". Have an adult put two more beans in the oven for 10 seconds. Plant them in the "10"-second egg carton pockets. Do the same thing for 15, 20, and 25 seconds. Plant the beans in the right holes.

We are planting two seeds instead of just one to give us a true test. Not all seeds "germinate," or begin to grow. Sometimes there may be something wrong with a seed and it won't germinate. By planting more than one seed each time, there is a better chance of a successful test.

Pour water onto the beans. Be sure they are thoroughly wet, but not swimming in water. Close the lid of the egg carton to keep the seeds moist. Check them each day and add water equally to all the seeds if they look dry. Write down what you see each day. What do you think will happen? Hypothesize that the seeds that were in the oven the longest will not germinate. (A hypothesis is one possible answer, or guess, based on what you know. The hypothesis must be tried and tested to see if it is true.)

After two weeks, look at your results and see if your hypothesis was right.

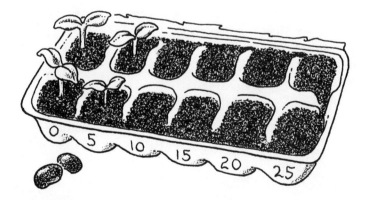

Something more
Try other fast-sprouting seeds, such as peas or radish seeds. Do the test using bulb plants.

Project 108
FADE OUT
How sunlight affects colors

A sunny window is a great place to put a plant, but it might not be a good place to put your couch. Plants do well in sunlight, but how do couches do? What if sunlight does something to the color of cloth. Hypothesize that sunlight can fade the color of things.

Gather two pieces of red, orange, yellow, green, blue, and black construction paper. Cut two strips of red paper about 2 inches (5 cm) wide and 6 inches (15 cm) long. Cut two pieces each of orange, yellow, green, blue, and black the same length.

Using tape, stick one of each of the colored strips onto a window that gets a lot of sunlight. Take the other colored strips and place them in a dresser drawer, away from sunlight.

After two weeks, take the colored strips off the window. Take the other strips out of the dresser drawer. Set the strips next to each other, matching them by color. Can you see any difference between the colored strips that were kept in the

> **You need**
> - a sunny window
> - colored construction paper
> - adhesive tape
> - safety scissors
> - dresser drawer

drawer and the ones that were placed in the sunny window? Did any of the colors fade? Which color faded the most? Which color faded the least? If you put a couch in a sunny window, which color cloth do you think would be changed the least?

What would happen if the strips were left in the window for a month?

Something more

Gather two pieces of red, orange, yellow, green, blue, and black construction paper. Cut two strips of red paper about 2 inches (5 cm) wide and 6 inches (15 cm) long. Cut two pieces of orange, yellow, green, and blue the same length. With a black piece of construction paper, cut 5 strips 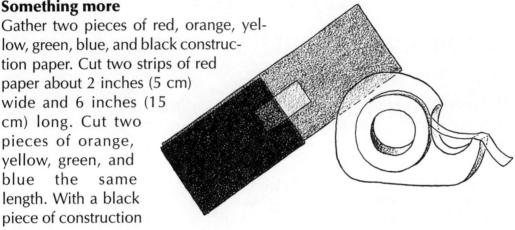 measuring 2 inches wide (5 cm) by 3 inches (8 cm) long. Take a black strip and tape it over half of the red strip. In the same way, tape a black piece of paper over half of the orange, yellow, green, and blue strips. Half of each colored strip will be visible and half will be covered by black paper. Using tape, stick these strips on a window that gets a lot of sun. The side of the strips that have the black paper on them should be facing outside. Take the other colored strips and place them in a dresser drawer, away from sunlight.

After two weeks, take the colored strips off the window. Take the strips out of the dresser drawer. Set the strips next to each other, matching them by color. Take the black strips off. Can you see any difference in the colored strips that were kept in the drawer and the ones that were placed in the sunny window? Is there any difference between the parts of the colored strips that were covered by the black paper and the colored paper kept in the drawer? Did any colors fade even though they were covered by black paper?

How do other colors, like brown, purple, and white, do in sunlight?

Project 109
BLOWING IN THE WIND
Comparing evaporation indoors and out

All plants must have a certain amount of water. to grow. Garden plants, that live outdoors, may need to be watered more often than plants that are always indoors. A garden may need water more often than potted plants. The sun and the air outside dry the soil. Hypothesize that soil dries more quickly outdoors than indoors.

Check the weather forecast. The next two days will need to be sunny.

Fill two empty one-pound plastic butter tubs with potting soil. Leave the soil loose in the tub. Do not pack it down. Use a small food scale or a balance beam to see that the containers weigh the same (You can make a simple balance beam by laying a ruler across a pencil, or hanging a coat hanger from a string and then using a paper clip at each end to hold light materials.) If one container is heavier, scoop a little of the potting soil out with a spoon until the tubs and their soil weigh the same.

> **You need**
> - 2 one-pound plastic butter tubs
> - potting soil
> - measuring cup
> - food scale
> - 2 sunny days
> - water
> - a sunny window

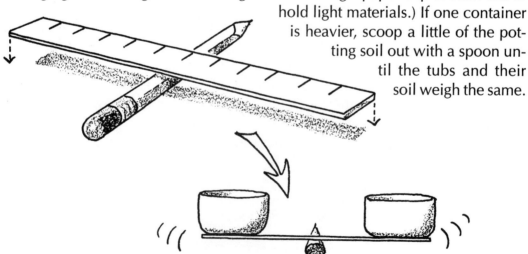

Fill a kitchen measuring cup with water to $\frac{1}{2}$ cup. Pour all of the water into one tub. Fill the measuring cup again to $\frac{1}{2}$ cup. Pour all of the water into the other tub.

Put one tub outside your house in the sun. On the same side of the house, put the other tub inside in a sunny window.

At the end of two days, weigh each of the tubs on the kitchen scale or compare them using a balance beam. The lighter tub will have had more water dry out of it.

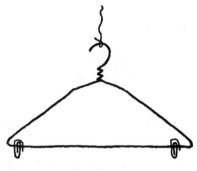

Something more
Is there any difference if the days are cloudy? Does it make a difference if the wind is calm or strong?

Project 110
SHAKE, RATTLE, & GERMINATE
Breaking down seed coats

Many seeds have a coat covering them. Often, before a seed can germinate and start to grow, its hard coat needs to be weakened or broken down. Hypothesize that seeds whose coats have been weakened by scratching will start to grow before seeds that are not scratched.

Ask an adult to cut out two round pieces of rough sandpaper using old scissors. Glue one piece to the inside bottom of a plastic butter tub or margarine container, and the other piece inside the tub's lid.

You need
- a one-pound plastic butter tub
- sandpaper (80 grit)
- old scissors
- an adult to cut sandpaper
- bean seeds
- watch or clock with a second hand
- potting soil
- 4 egg cartons
- glue
- marking pen
- water
- pencil and paper

Next, fill six pockets in each of four egg cartons with potting soil. Put six beans in the soil in one egg carton. Each seed should be planted in its own separate pocket. Use a marking pen to write "Not shaken" on the top of the egg carton.

Place six other bean seeds inside the tub with the sandpaper. Shake the tub as hard as you can for ten seconds. Put the seeds in an egg carton. Write "Shaken 10 seconds" on the lid of the carton.

Put six bean seeds inside the tub and shake as hard as you can for 30 seconds. Plant these seeds in another egg carton and write "Shaken 30 seconds" on the lid. Do the same thing for 60 seconds. Write the time on the lid of the egg carton.

Sprinkle water on all of the seeds. Close the lids to keep them from drying out.

Every day, open the lids and see if any seeds have begun to grow. Write down on the paper the date and anything you observe. If the potting soil feels dry, water all the seeds equally.

After one or two weeks, look at your notes. Which seeds began to grow first? Did the shaking cause any of the seeds not to grow at all?

Something more

Will the results be the same for all seeds? Try morning glory, radish, and other kinds of flower or vegetable seeds.

Does soaking in water, tea, or other liquid affect how fast seeds germinate? Soak some seeds for one day, soak others for three days, and others for five days.

Project 111
YOU BUG ME
Attracting insects to sweetened liquids

All of us have seen flying insects gather around a porch light at night during the warm and hot times of the year. We know that many insects are attracted to light. Are there other things that attract them? Do they like sweet things? Hypothesize that they do.

Get four small cereal bowls: they must all be the same size. Pour soda into one bowl. Pour milk into another bowl. Pour water into the third bowl. Pour pancake syrup into the last bowl.

When night comes, put the four bowls on a table outdoors, underneath a porch light. The bright light will attract insects to the table. After one hour, look at the four bowls. Count the number of insects you see in and around the edge of each bowl. Are there more insects at the sweet pancake syrup and soda bowls than there are at the milk and water bowls?

You need
- porch with a light
- 4 cereal bowls
- picnic table
- pancake syrup
- soda
- milk
- a warm night

Something more
Get a book on insects. Can you identify any of the insects that visited your bowls?

Project 112
JUST A DRINK OF WATER
Moisture needed to germinate seeds

A seed needs water to germinate, but how much water does a bean seed need? Hypothesize that if a seed does not get enough water, it will not begin to grow. This often happens in nature, if there is not enough rain or the air is too dry.

With a marking pen, write the numbers 1 through 12 on an egg carton, putting one number near each pocket that normally holds an egg. Fill all 12 pockets with potting soil. Put one bean seed in each pocket.

You need
- eyedropper
- bean seeds
- water
- plastic or plastic-foam egg carton
- potting soil
- marking pen
- pencil and paper

Fill an eyedropper with water. Every morning at the same time, such as 8 o'clock, put one drop of water on the seed marked "1", two drops of water on the seed marked "2", three drops on the seed marked "3", and so on. Always leave the lid of the egg carton open. Do this again twelve hours later, at 8 o'clock in the evening. Water the beans in this way every day for two weeks. Look at the project every day and write down what happens. At the end of the two weeks, see which seeds germinated. Did the seeds that were given only a few drops of water a day germinate?

Something more

Do the same project again, but this time use two egg cartons with seeds. Keep the lids closed on them. (Closing the lid should help keep in warmth and moisture.) Put one carton of seeds in a sunny window and the other in a dark place.

Project 113
BANANA COOKER
Ripening fruit by heat and light

People sometimes put fruit and vegetables in a sunny window to make them ripen faster. Is it the light from the sun or its warmth that causes them to ripen? Choose which you think is right.

Take two shoe boxes Paint the outside of one box with black paint. Paint the outside of the other shoe box white. Let the boxes dry. Place the two shoe boxes in a sunny window. Put one green banana in each box. Place a thermometer next to each banana. Put the lids on. Put the last banana on the window,sill with a thermometer next to it.

Look at the temperature on the thermometers four times a day: when you get up, at lunchtime, before dinner, and at bedtime. Pick them up by the tube to read them. Be careful not to touch the metal tip or you will change the temperature. Write down the readings.

You need
- 3 green (unripe) bananas
- 3 thermometers
- 2 shoeboxes
- black paint
- white paint
- paintbrush
- a sunny window
- pencil and paper

Do this every day for two or three days. Look at the bananas. Are all the bananas turning yellow at the same time? Touch them. Is one softer than the others? Do you think softer means riper?

Something more
Do some of the yellow bananas have many black spots on the skin? Do the black spots mean that the banana has gone bad? Peel the three bananas and taste and compare them Are they different?

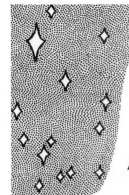

Project 114
NIGHT SKY
A matter of seeing stars

Before the invention of the telescope in the early 1600s, the naked eye was the only tool people had to study and learn about the night sky. How many stars can you see, without using a telescope or binoculars?

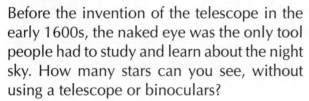

You need
- a clear, dark night (no bright moon or lights)
- some friends
- large bowls or jars
- large bag of beans
- pencil and paper

On a nice night, without clouds or a bright moon, take blankets or sleeping bags, large containers (one per friend), and beans, and go outside. The area should be as dark as possible, so turn off any outdoor lights you can. Wait ten minutes or so for your eyes to adjust to the darkness, then lie on your back and look up at the stars.

First, decide where you are going to begin counting. You do not want to take your eyes away from the sky while you are counting or you will lose your place. Then, drop a bean into a bowl for each star you see. When you have counted all the stars you can see, take out the beans and count them.

How many stars did you count? Write it down. How many stars did each of your friends count? Have another star-count outing on a night when the moon is full. Compare how many stars you can count.

Something more
How do the bright lights from neighbors' houses, or in small towns or big cities, affect the number of stars you can see? Do you think light pollution is a problem for astronomers? What can they do about it? Read a book about the large telescopes and find out where they are located. Maybe you can visit one.

After being outside in the dark for a while, go into a bright room in the house. After a few minutes, go back outside. How long does it take for your eyes to adjust to the dark again?

Project 115
BACKYARD FORECASTER
Predicting weather by wind direction

Some people use a barometer, an instrument that measures air pressure, to help forecast the weather. When the barometer's needle is rising, fair weather is usually coming. When the needle falls, rain is likely.

What about wind direction? Hypothesize that wind direction can also be used to indicate fair or stormy weather, then test it out.

Find an area in your yard or other place nearby where there is nothing to block the wind. Hammer the wooden stake a little way

You need
- a long thin strip of lightweight cloth
- a wooden stake about 4 feet (120 cm) long
- hammer
- magnetic compass
- thumbtack
- a week or two
- outside area
- pencil and paper
- bright-colored yarn
- 4 ice-cream sticks

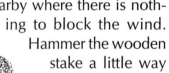

into the ground, until it stands up securely. Using a thumbtack, fasten one end of a thin strip of cloth to the top of the stake.

Standing at the stake, use a magnetic compass to find north, south, east, and west. Mark a direction—N, S, E, and W—at the tip of each ice-cream stick, then push them into the ground about three feet (90 cm) from the stake in each of the four directions. Tie a piece of bright-colored yarn around the stake and out to the ice-cream stick to the north (N). Do the same for the other three directions. This will help you see the wind direction from a distance.

Every day, once in the morning and again in the evening, look to see which direction the wind is blowing the cloth. You need to record the wind direction on both fair days and stormy days. After a few weeks, examine your log to see the wind direction you recorded just before a storm and just before fair weather. Was your hypothesis correct?

Something more
Can you use your ribbon device to measure wind speed? Make a scale showing wind speed. The ribbon is lifted farther away from the stick when the wind is blowing harder.

Project 116
TUNNELLERS
The digging habits of ants

You can always tell where there is an ant nest underground, by the telltale mound of soil around a small hole. In nature, many things can block an ant hole. An animal might walk over it and push soil into the hole. A tree limb may fall during a storm and cover the entrance to the ants' nest.

What do you think ants will do when their hole is covered? Will they dig the same hole out again, or will they make a new hole near the old one? Hypothesize which you think will happen.

Find five ant hills. Put a handful of soil over each hole. Do not harm any of the ants. Keep checking around the holes. Write down anything you see the ants doing. If the ants do the same thing at each hole, can you guess where the ants would dig if you covered another hole?

What if a very small twig or piece of straw were placed in the opening of an ant hole? Would the ants try to move it? Could they? What does that tell you about ants?

Something more

Do you think that ants have more than one way of getting in and out of their underground homes? Build an ant farm, or buy one; then watch to see if the ants make more than one opening into their home.

You need
- 5 ant hills
- pencil and paper

186

Project 117
CLIP IN A BOTTLE
Comparing force fields

We are all familiar with the force of gravity and magnetic force. When a magnet is brought near something metal, the magnet tries to pull the metal object to it. When you try to jump up, the force of gravity pulls you back down towards the Earth. The force of gravity and magnetic force are invisible forces, but they are very strong. Can a magnetic force be stronger than gravity?

Have an adult poke a small hole in the lid of a clear glass jar, such as a mayonnaise jar or a jar that held apple sauce.

Turn the jar upside down and use adhesive tape to stick a magnet onto the bottom of the jar. The magnet should be on the outside of the jar.

Tie one end of a piece of thread to the small end of a safety pin. Push the other end up through the bottom of the lid. Screw the lid onto the jar. Slowly pull the thread up through the hole until the safety pin is standing straight up, with its tip just touching the bottom of the jar. Put a piece of adhesive tape over the hole in the lid to keep the hanging safety pin in place.

Slowly turn the jar over and place it upside down on its lid. Does the magnetic force keep the safety pin in place, or does gravity make it fall down?

You need
- an adult
- a hammer
- safety pin
- clear glass jar with lid
- strong magnet
- thread
- adhesive tape

Something more
Will a stronger magnet allow you to raise the safety pin off of the bottom of the jar? How high off the bottom of the jar can you raise it and still have the magnetic force strong enough to overcome gravity?

Project 118
EARLY RISERS
Animal sounds, day and night

Some animals sleep during the day and are awake at night. Others sleep at night and are active during the day. Animal sounds can be heard outside at any time: owls, birds, raccoons, frogs, crickets, locusts, cats, dogs, horses, cows, ducks. Hypothesize that the animal sounds that are heard in the morning are not the same as the ones heard after dark.

Early in the morning, after the sun has risen, go outside, announce the time of day for the tape recorder and then record about five minutes of animal sounds. In the evening, after dark, announce the time again and then record another five minutes of animal sounds.

Listen to the recordings you made. Are the animal sounds recorded in the morning the same as the ones heard at night? Make a list of the animal sounds you recorded.

> **You need**
> - outside
> - tape recorder
> - pencil and paper

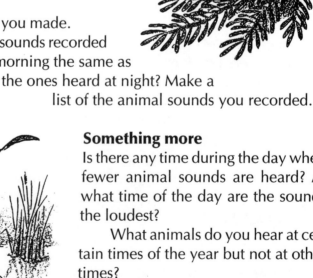

Something more
Is there any time during the day when fewer animal sounds are heard? At what time of the day are the sounds the loudest?

What animals do you hear at certain times of the year but not at other times?

Project 119
COOL SMELLS
The effect of temperature on odors

A molecule is a very tiny particle of matter made up of groups of even tinier particles called atoms. Molecules move faster when they are heated than when they are cold. As the temperature increases, more molecules escape and travel into the air. This means that perfume molecules can be smelled more easily when the perfume is warmed, as when you put some on your skin.

Since molecules move more slowly when they are cold, hypothesize that perfume will not smell as strong if it is cold.

Tear a sheet of paper towel into three strips. Fold each strip three or four times, to make it thicker. Put three drops of perfume on each piece. Leave one section of towel on the table, at room temperature. Place another towel section in the refrigerator, and the last piece in the freezer. After several hours, use your nose to test which of the three perfumed pieces of toweling has the strongest smell

You need
- paper towel
- perfume
- use of a refrigerator
- use of a freezer

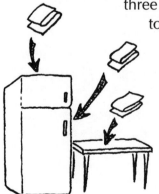

Something more
What do you think would happen if you were to put the perfumed toweling from the freezer into a sunny window? Would molecules of garlic juice, lemon juice, and other "smelly" things react in the same way to heat and cold?

Project 120
BOXED-IN
A characteristic of recycled cardboard

You need
- a variety of food boxes (cereal, noodles, sugar, pudding, crackers, etc.)
- pencil and paper

Because they are concerned about the environment, many companies are using recycled cardboard and paper to make packaging for their products. Some boxes with the recycled symbol on them are light in color. Hypothesize that recycled "paperboard" is generally lighter in color than non-recycled cardboard.

Gather many different kinds of food boxes, such as contain noodles, sugar, gelatin, pudding, pretzels, and pet food. On a piece of paper write the name of the product. Note whether or not the box is made

of recycled paperboard (it will be marked on the box if it is), and if the color of the box is light or dark. Since the outside of the package will likely have printing on it, open the box and look on the inside, where there is no printing.

Go over your notes. Did you find that all or most of the packages made from recycled paperboard were lighter in color? Did you find some boxes that didn't say they were recycled also had cardboard that was light in color?

SPAGHETTI - dark
CAT FOOD - light
CORNFLAKES - dark
SUGAR - light
SODA -
COCOA -
RICE MIX -

Something more
Research what "recycled" means in making packaging. Is it made of all recycled material, or is there only *some* recycled material in it?

Write to a company that does not use recycled material in their packaging and ask them to do it.

Project 121
ROCK COLLECTION, CITY-STYLE

Grouping rocks by their characteristics

Rocks are just about everywhere. If you live in the city or on the plains, you may still find a lot of different types of rocks in your community because people have brought them into your neighborhood. Rocks may be brought in from outside your neighborhood to make driveways, rock gardens, home decorations, landscaping, drainage, monuments, and building structures (like granite for stairs).

You need
- 20 different types of rocks from your neighborhood
- library books on rocks and minerals
- pencil and paper

Gather 20 or more different types of rocks from your neighborhood. Identify the rocks by using a book from the library, asking a science teacher, or asking anyone who knows about rocks.

Group them by hardness. Remember, you can determine if one rock is harder than another by trying to scratch one rock with another. The one that makes the scratch is harder than the one that gets scratched.

Something more

Are there any other characteristics about the rocks you have collected that are interesting? Are some rocks smooth? Why might that be?

Project 122
ARE ALL CANS CREATED EQUAL?
Comparing soda containers

Years ago, soda came in very thick and heavy glass bottles. Today, glass and other packaging materials are costly and we don't want to waste them, so soda comes in thinner glass bottles, plastic bottles, and thin aluminum cans that are recycled.

Do the makers of aluminum soda cans all use the same amount of aluminum in their products, or are some cans heavier than others? Do the manufacturers of 2-liter soda bottles all use the same quantity of plastic in their bottles?

Form a hypothesis, then collect 10 different brands of aluminum soda cans (leave the flip-tops on). Rinse out the cans and let them dry completely. Weigh each can on a scale and record the results. (If you don't have a gram-weight or postal/food scale, place two thumbtacks side by side, with the points up. Lay a ruler across them, so that the ruler balances like a seesaw. Place two cans, in turn, one on each end of the ruler, and see which is heavier).

Which of the cans is the heaviest? Which one is the lightest? If you have a scale, subtract the weight of the lightest can from the weight of the heaviest. Is there a big difference, or very little difference?

Something more

Do the same thing with plastic soda bottles. Is there a bigger difference between the weights of the bottles or the weights of the cans?

You need
- 10 same-size aluminum soda cans (12 ounces), all different brands
- 10 2-liter soda bottles, all different brands
- scale or homemade balance
- pencil and paper

Project 123
A BETTER BATTER?
Why some foods hold heat

Some foods cool very quickly after being cooked or heated. Toast cools very fast, but a potato stays hot for a long time. Why?

If thicker foods hold their warmth longer than thinner ones, a thicker pancake should keep its heat longer than a thin one. Ask an adult to help you do this recipe experiment.

Mix two bowls of pancake batter. Make one batter thicker. Add more milk to make the second batter thinner. Then, into a frying pan or on a grill, measure the same amount of each batter. Make one pancake using thick batter and the other using thin batter.

> **You need**
> - an adult, to make pancakes
> - stove or grill
> - utensils (spoon, knife, mixing bowls, frying pan)
> - pancake mix
> - milk
> - stick of margarine
> - 2 dinner plates

When both pancakes are all cooked, put each one on a plate. Cut two same size $1/4$-inch slices from a stick of margarine that has been left at room temperature. Put one slice in the middle of each pancake. Watch the margarine. Does the slice pat on the thicker pancake melt faster than the one on the thin pancake?

Something more
Which cooked foods cool fastest after being served? Which foods stay hot the longest? Can anything be done to help keep foods warm longer? Will warming the plate before putting a pancake on it help to keep the pancake warm longer? Should syrup, honey, or jelly be warmed before putting it onto a pancake?

Project 124
TAMPER CHECK
Consumer safety awareness

Because something you eat or drink can be bad for you, food manufacturers list every ingredient on their packaging. All the ingredients have been tested, and are safe for most people to eat.

You need
- a variety of packaged goods from the grocery store (peanut butter, vitamins, bottled soda, etc.)
- pencil and paper

To keep people from opening up and tampering with foods before they are brought home, many companies make their packaging tamper-resistant. This makes the products safer to use. It also sometimes helps to keep foods fresher, so that they last longer.

The next time groceries are brought into your home, help to unpack them and check each item to see if it has any special packaging to help make it hard to tamper with. Peanut butter jars often have a foil seal under the lid. (There should be no pin holes or other breaks in the seal.) A vitamin bottle may have an extra plastic collar around the screw-off cap, in addition to the foil seal. The collar of a soda bottle cape is made to separate when the bottle is opened. (Soda bottles also make a loud hissing or fizzing sound when they are opened for the first time.) Cans that are vacuum-packed for freshness, like peanuts, might make a "popping" sound when they are fist opened. Jellies and other products vacuum-packed in glass jars often have bubble caps. The middle of the cap pops up when the vacuum is broken, so it is easy to see if the jar has been opened.

Look, listen, feel, and examine each product. Make a chart and write down the name of the product and how it is made tamper-resistant.

Something more
What should you do if you find something that might have been tampered with?

194

Project 125
DYEING TO STAIN
Coloring with natural dyes

Dyes are used to color things. We can get many dyes from nature.

Get four small plastic butter or margarine tubs. Pour purple grape juice in one tub, cherry juice in another, and cranberry juice in the third tub. In the fourth tub, put in a teabag and pour warm water over it. Let it sit for 15 minutes.

Cut strips of cloth out of an old tee shirt or bed sheet. Dip one piece of cloth in each tub of natural dye. Use clothes pin to hang the strips on a clothesline to dry. Be careful handling them. You wouldn't want to stain your clothes.

Use your colored strips when you work on arts and crafts projects.

Can you find other things in nature that can be used as dyes? Try the purple berries of poke weed or other plants you have in your neighborhood.

> **You need**
> - pieces of old cloth
> - teabag
> - cranberry juice
> - cherry juice
> - purple grape juice
> - 4 small plastic butter or margarine tubs
> - warm water
> - clothesline and clothespins

Something more
What cultures used natural dyes? In some cultures, people paint their faces. What do they use for paint?

Project 126
SPLISH-SPLASH IT OUT!

Understanding soil erosion

Have you ever started to water a flower bed but forgot to put the sprinkler on the end of the garden hose? If the water was turned on full force, soil probably splashed out of the flower bed, leaving big holes. That is why sprinkling cans and sprinkler hose attachments, with many small holes, are used to water pots of flowers and outside gardens.

Erosion, or the wearing away of soil, is caused by water travelling fast, as it does during a heavy downpour. Erosion is often especially bad on a hillside. Hypothesize that the faster water is travelling, the more erosion damage it can do.

Fill three small bowls evenly with cereal flakes, all the way to the top. Fill a half-gallon pitcher with water. Find a small stairway outside your home; you need at least five steps. Place a bowl of cereal on the ground at the end of the first step. Set the pitcher on that step, near the edge, and slowly tip it towards the bowl so the water falls from that height, lands in the bowl of cereal, and splashes some of the cereal out.

Fill the pitcher with water again. Place another bowl of cereal alongside the third step on the staircase. Set the pitcher on the edge of the third step and slowly tip it so that the water will again fall into the bowl.

196

Do this one more time, only put the pitcher on the fifth step.

Gravity makes things fall faster. The farther something falls, the faster it goes. Water poured from the fifth step will fall faster than water poured from the first step when it hits the bowl.

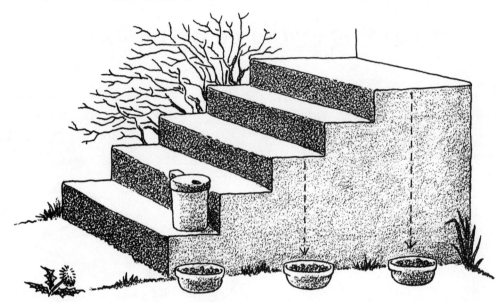

Look at each of the cereal bowls. In which one did the most "erosion" (loss of cereal) take place?

If your stairway has more than five steps, you can try pouring water from an even greater height.

If you wish, you can quantify, or measure, the amount of cereal that splashes out at each height by catching it in a tray or cookie sheet. Then let the cereal dry out and weigh it.

Leave the cereal used in this project as a treat for your neighborhood birds, squirrels, and chipmunks.

Something more
Put soil into a bowl or tray and place it under a downspout. What happens to the soil during a rainstorm? Try other kinds of soil. Is there a difference in the way it erodes?

Project 127
WEAR, WHERE?
Finding evidence of friction

Erosion is when soil wears away, usually caused by wind or moving water. Things can be worn away by friction, too. When two materials rub against each other, the friction from the movement can wear away the materials.

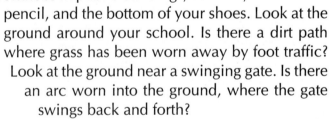

You need
- your neighborhood
- pencil and paper

Look around your home, school, and neighborhood to find evidence of wear. Make a chart and list the things that you find that show wear. Write down where you find the wear, and make a guess as to what caused it. For example, at the public library, look at the steps. Do you seen any difference on the part of the steps where people normally walk? Would you guess that the wear on the steps is caused by the friction of people's shoes on the steps? Look for wear on hand railings, floors, carpeting, doorknobs in public buildings, car tires, the end of a pencil, and the bottom of your shoes. Look at the ground around your school. Is there a dirt path where grass has been worn away by foot traffic? Look at the ground near a swinging gate. Is there an arc worn into the ground, where the gate swings back and forth?

Something more

Do a "wear" report and share it with your classmates.

Project 128
DRIED OUT
Surface area and evaporation

Water evaporates, or disappears, into the air. The wet dew that collects on the grass in the morning usually evaporates by noon on a sunny day. How long would a cup of water take to evaporate? That depends on such things as the movement of the air and its dryness and temperature. But, those things being the same, the amount of the water's surface exposed to the air, called the "surface area," makes a big difference in evaporation time. If a cup of water is poured into a pie plate, were it can spread out, it will evaporate much faster than if the same amount of water is poured into a soda bottle that only has a small opening at the top.

> **You need**
> • measuring cup
> • soda bottle
> • pie plate
> • water
> • a sunny window

Using a measuring cup, pour one-half cup of water into a soda bottle and one-half cup of water into a pie plate. Place them on a table by a sunny window. Several times a day, look at each one. Which is the first to become completely dry?

Something more
Using three pie plates, set up an experiment to discover which evaporates faster: water, soda, or juice.

Project 129
COLOR ME HOT
Changing solar heating with color

The sun's light is energy that makes heat. When sunlight hits a dark object, much of the light is trapped. This makes the object warmer. When sunlight hits something light it bounces off (is reflected) and very little of the heat is trapped.

Fill the five drinking glasses with water. Each glass should be filled to the same level.

Choose five different-colored pieces of construction paper. One piece should be white, and one piece black. The other three pieces can be any other solid colors.

Wrap some black construction paper around one glass of water. Tape it in place. Then tape a piece of white construction paper around another glass and tape it. Wrap a different-colored paper around each of the other three glasses. Put the wrapped glasses of water in a sunny window. After about an hour of sun, put a thermometer in the first glass of water. Wait about three minutes, then read the temperature. Write it down. Measure the water temperature in each of the other glasses and write that down too.

Is the water in the glasses covered by the dark paper warmer? Which is the warmest? Which glass has the water that is coolest?

You need
- 5 straight-sided glasses (same size)
- water
- construction paper (white, black, and others)
- adhesive tape
- a sunny window
- thermometer

Something more
Will a dark-colored liquid heat faster than a light-colored liquid? Use room-temperature milk and coffee, or add food coloring to water.

200

Project 130
RAINBOW FRUIT
Decorating with food

Color is very important in our lives. Colors are everywhere. Brightly colored packaging is used by manufacturers to make us want to buy their products. Even our emotions and moods can be changed by colors.

People use certain colors for holiday decorations. Black and orange are for Halloween. Green and red are Christmas colors. Light blue and light pink are for Easter. Can fruit be colored to make it fit the holiday?

Put a slice of banana, apple, peach, pineapple, and kiwi on a plate. Place a few drops of food coloring on each piece of fruit. Are any of the pieces of fruit easy to change their color? Try to color slices of other kinds of fresh fruits. Can you make a decorative plate of fruit slices for the next holiday?

> **You need**
> • slice of banana
> • slice of apple
> • slice of peach
> • slice of pineapple
> • slice of kiwifruit
> • food coloring
> • dinner plate

Something more
Can vegetables be colored with food coloring, too? Can you make a blue carrot or a green potato?

Write "Happy Birthday" on a banana, by slicing it along its length (the long way) and dipping a toothpick in food coloring to use as a pen. The toothpick will etch the letters into the banana.

The writing can be done either in dots, in lines, or both.

Project 131
LENDING LIBRARY
Recycling and extending the life of toys

If something can be used more than only once before throwing it away, it will help to reduce the amount of trash taken to landfills. Have your teacher set up a shelf in the classroom as a "lending library." Classmates can bring in books and games to lend to others. (Be sure the name of the person it belongs to is marked on each item, so that it can be returned.)

Some good items for the lending library are video-game cartridges (Nintendo®, Atari®, and others), books, comics, magazines, computer games, and videotapes. Classmates should ask their parents first if the item can be brought in to the lending library.

Passing along to others things that we don't use anymore will help the environment by cutting down on what is thrown away. Extending the life of what we have will cut down on the number of new things we need to buy, and therefore need to manufacture, saving the Earth's resources.

You need
- items collected from friends
- pencil and paper

Something more

Extend the life of things by repairing them. Start a toy repair shop in your classroom, where broken trucks and torn teddy bears can be fixed. Outgrown or unwanted toys can be donated.

Project 132
FIZZ MYSTERY
The secret that is soda

Did you ever taste "flat" soda? Soda that has lost its fizz, does not bubble anymore, is called flat. The people who make soda add the bubbles to make the soda taste better. The bubbles come from a gas called carbon dioxide. As long as the cap is screwed on the soda bottle tight, or the can is unopened, the carbon dioxide stays inside the soda and keeps it tasting fizzy good.

Does freezing soda and then thawing it cause the carbon dioxide gas to leave the soda and make it go flat? Put a can of soda in the freezer. Leave it there for only two hours, long enough for the soda to begin to freeze. (We don't want to really freeze the whole can of soda, because the water in the soda expands when it freezes and could break the can open!) Remember to take the soda out of the freezer after two hours or you may always remember the mess it makes!

Place the cold soda on a table, but not in sunlight. Put an identical can of soda next to it. After four hours, open the two soda cans and pour each one into a large glass. Does one have more fizz and foam than the other?

Something more

Can you stir the gas out of a soda? Some people do not like a lot of fizz, because the gas is released later in their stomachs and causes discomfort. Is there something you can put into the soda to get the gas out?

Did you ever drop or shake a can of soda and then open it? The soda shoots out very quickly! After a can of soda is shaken, how long do you have to wait before it is safe to open it without worrying about the soda shooting out?

Project 133
LEFTOVER SALT
Collecting salt from ocean waters

Our oceans are full of salt. If you were out on the ocean in a little boat and were thirsty, you would not be able to drink the ocean water. The salt in it would only make you more thirsty. In some places in the world, oceans dried up long ago and left the salt behind.

Hypothesize that you can show how salt is left when saltwater evaporates. Have an adult help you measure $\frac{1}{4}$ cup of hot tap water and pour it into a wide-mouth drinking glass. Measure and pour another $\frac{1}{4}$ cup of hot water into another wide-mouth glass. Into one glass, pour $\frac{1}{2}$ teaspoon of salt. Stir it. Place both glasses in a sunny window. Each day, look at the two glasses and write down what you see. Is something building up on the bottom of the glass of saltwater?

You need
- $\frac{1}{2}$ teaspoon measure
- measuring cup
- an adult
- hot water from a sink
- salt
- 2 wide-mouth drinking glasses
- a sunny window
- pencil and paper

Something more
Use the evaporation process to remove salt from the water of a saltwater lake, river, or ocean nearby. Pour some of the salty water on a cookie sheet. When the water you poured has evaporated, pour more of it onto the sheet. Keep adding more water, as the water on the cookie sheet evaporates. You will soon see salt from the water slowly begin to build up on the sheet.

Project 134
FREEZE OR DON'T?
Preserving with cold

Preserving foods means doing something to make them stay fresh longer. Many foods can be kept fresher for a longer time if they are stored where it is cold. Milk stays fresh much longer if it is stored in a refrigerator than if it is left on the kitchen table.

Some foods are preserved by freezing them. Look in your refrigerator's freezer and see what is being stored in it. You may find ice-cream, meat, and vegetables such as frozen peas, carrots, corn, and lima beans.

What about other kinds of food? Can we use freezing to keep all foods, or just certain kinds? Let's do a test.

Put a fresh piece of carrot in a small, plastic food bag. Put a fresh piece of lettuce in another small plastic bag. Put a fresh piece of celery in a plastic food bag. Place the three bags in a freezer. Leave them there for a day or two.

Remove them from the freezer, and let them thaw out for a few hours. Then look at them carefully; touch them and taste them. Write down any changes you see and any difference in taste caused by the freezing. Is the lettuce still as crisp as it was before it was frozen? Do you think freezing is a good way to keep these vegetables longer?

Something more
Try to preserve other foods by freezing, such as an egg. Put it into a plastic bag to keep the freezer clean in case it should break. Try to freeze pieces of fruit.

Project 135
GARBAGE HELPERS
Decomposition by tiny animals

Big animals, little animals, and even animals so tiny we can't see them with our naked eyes eat food and help break it down. After your family has eaten a chicken dinner, take two similar leftover bones (such as drumsticks or thigh bones) that still have some chicken on them. Put one leftover chicken bone in a plastic sandwich bag and store it in a freezer. Put the other one on the ground outside of your house. It should be in a place where no one will disturb it. Cover the chicken bone by placing a colander upside down on top of it. Put a heavy brick on top of the colander to help keep cats and dogs away from it.

After a few weeks, look at the chicken bone under the colander. Do not touch it. Use a clothespin to hold it up and look at it. Compare it to the one that was kept in the freezer. Which one decomposed, broke down, or rotted faster? Did you see any small animals (ants, flies, etc.) eating from the chicken bone that was left outside?

You need
- 2 chicken bones with scraps on them
- colander
- brick
- clothespin
- plastic sandwich bag
- refrigerator freezer

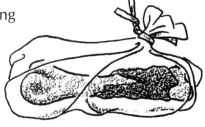

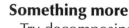

Something more
Try decomposing other types of food like celery, potatoes, radishes, and a piece of bread. Put some in the freezer, some on the ground, and bury some.

Project 136
SMART SPROUTS
Vegetables that start growing by themselves

Plants need moisture and food to grow. Some vegetables, like onions and potatoes, have inside of them everything they need to start growing— all by themselves.

Put two fresh onions and two fresh potatoes in a shoe box. Put the lid tightly on the shoe box so that it is dark inside. Find a cool, out-of-the-way place in your home to put the box, such as your bedroom closet. At the end of one week, open the box. Carefully look at the vegetables. Can you see any changes? Write down what you see.

Put the lid back on the box and wait another week. Then look at the vegetables again. Now what do you see? Write it down. Look at the vegetables every week for four weeks, and write down what happens to them

> **You need**
> • 2 fresh onions
> • 2 fresh potatoes
> • a shoe box with lid
> • 4 weeks' time
> • pencil and paper

Something more
A carrot has food inside of it, but often not enough water

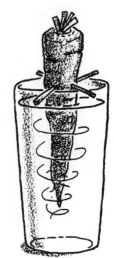

for the carrot to grow on its own. It needs a little help.

Take a fresh carrot and push four toothpicks partway into it, around the middle. Pour some water in a tall glass. Place the carrot in the glass so that the toothpicks rest on the rim and keep it from falling in. Be sure there is always enough water in the glass to reach the bottom of the carrot.

Project 137
TEA TAMPERING
Changing the pH of tea

Many people like to drink tea. Some like lemon in their tea, others like milk. Does adding milk to tea make it less likely to upset your stomach? It might, if adding milk changes the amount of acid in tea and makes it milder.

The amount of acid in a liquid is measured by "pH". The pH scale goes from 1 to 9: the lower the number, the stronger the acid.

First, pour a glass of water from your sink. Use litmus paper to find out the pH of your water. Write it down.

Then have an adult help you make a cup of tea. Use litmus paper to find out how much acid (called tannic acid) is in the tea. Write the amount down.

Add milk to the tea and stir. Now check the pH of the tea again. Does adding milk raise the pH and make the tea less acidy? If the pH of the tea is raised, do you think the tea would be less likely to upset your stomach? What is the pH of milk?

> **You need**
> - a glass of water
> - litmus paper with a pH scale of 3 to 8
> - an adult
> - a cup of tea
> - milk

Something more
What is the pH of tea with lemon? What is the pH of different kinds of soda?

Project 138
ROCK & ROLL-OVER
Looking at life under rocks

What kinds of living things make their homes under rocks? Find out by turning over several large rocks in your neighborhood. You may find ants, larvae, worms, millipedes (many legs), centipedes (a hundred legs), spiders, crickets, or beetles; but watch out for creatures that bite or sting.

Draw pictures of the animals you find living under the rocks. Describe their body parts, the number of legs they have, their coloring, and other things about them. Get a book on insects from the library and try to identify the animals you saw. If some of the rocks you looked under were in a wet place, such as near a lake, and some in a dry place, did you find different kinds of animals under each, or the same kinds?

You need
- several large rocks in your neighborhood
- a strong stick
- an adult
- pencil and paper

Something more
Are the animals that you find under a rock the same kind as those you find under an old board or log?

Camel Cricket
6 legs
dry
brown

Slug
no legs
wet
grey

Worm
no legs
damp
pinkish

Carrion Beetle
6 legs
damp
black

Scorpion
stings!

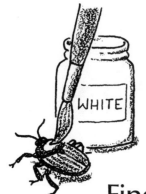

Project 139
TATTOOED TRAVELLERS
Finding out where insects live

You may have lifted an old board somewhere lying on the ground and seen some tiny animals (beetles, worms, etc.) crawling there. Is this their home, or are they just passing by? If it is their home, can they find their way back there if they are moved a short distance away?

Find an old board or a rock nearby that has been sitting on the ground for a long time. Lift it up carefully with the stick. Are there a number of tiny animals living there? Get a small craft paintbrush and a small bottle of white paint, the kind used for painting models. Use the brush to put one small drop of white paint on the back of any animals you see under the board. Put the board back in place.

The next day, look under the board again. Are the animals with the white markings still there? If they are, pick them up and place them on the ground a step or two away from the board. Put the board back. If you can't stay to watch, go back and lift up the board later on to see if they found their way back home.

Something more
Can you identify any of the kinds of animals that live under the board? Get a book on insects from the library.

Project 140
SALT-FREE
Water purification at home

Most of the oceans and seas in the world are made up of saltwater. When the water evaporates, salt is left behind so the ocean becomes even saltier. But is evaporated water still salty? Let's evaporate some saltwater, then bring the water back to see if it is salty, or if the salt is gone.

Ask an adult for a small clean can (the inside edge can be sharp where the lid was cut away, so you need to be careful). Fill the can about one-quarter full of salt. Add water to it until the can is three-quarters full. Stir it slowly until the salt is completely dissolved.

Take a large, wide-mouth jar: a mayonnaise or peanut butter jar works well. Clean the jar thoroughly; then, without spilling any of the saltwater, lower the can to the bottom of the jar. Screw the lid onto the jar tightly; this makes it a "closed environment."

Put the jar in a warm, sunny window for several hours. The sun's heat will cause water to evaporate. When the sun starts to go down, carefully place the still-closed jar in the refrigerator. The change in temperature from hot to cold will now make the evaporated moisture in the glass jar condense, and water droplets will collect on the inside of the jar. Open the jar, reach in, and taste the condensed droplets of water that have formed on the inside of it. Do you taste any salt, or does the water taste clean and pure?

You need
- an adult
- smallest-size, flat (tuna) can
- salt
- water
- spoon
- large, wide-mouth jar with lid
- a sunny window
- use of a refrigerator

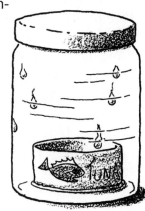

Something more
Can evaporation purify water, even if it is dirty instead of salty? Repeat the experiment above, but instead of mixing salt and water, mix a little soil into the water.

Project 141
TREES WITH RAINCOATS
Proving that tree leaves are waterproof

Trees get the water that they need to live through their roots deep in the ground. Even though rain falls on the leaves, trees do not get water through them. In fact, the tops of the leaves are waterproof. This also keeps the water already in the tree from evaporating. Can we prove that tree leaves are waterproof?

Stack some books on top of each other so that the pile is two to three inches (5–8 cm) high. Lay two rulers against the books to make a ramp. The rulers should be spaced three to four inches (8–10 cm) apart. Place a piece of paper towel underneath the ramp.

Gather about ten large tree leaves: broad ones like the leaves from sycamore or some oak trees. Lay the leaves down on the rulers, starting at the bottom of the ramp and overlapping the leaves as you go higher. The tops of the leaves on your ramp must face upward and their bottoms down. When you have completely covered the entire ramp with the over- lapping leaves, take a pencil or stick. Press it down between the rulers

> **You need**
> - several thick books
> - 10 large, broad tree leaves
> - 2 rulers
> - paper towel
> - small glass of water
> - a pencil or stick

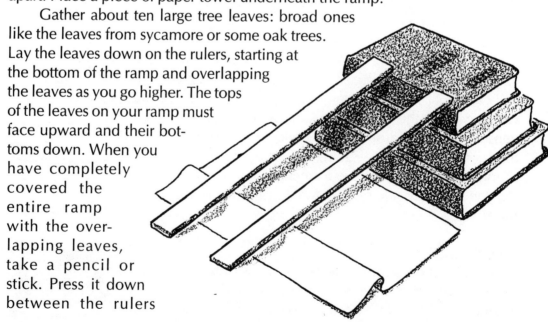

212

from the top to the bottom to make a little trough, or path, for the water to follow when you start to pour.

Place a few sheets of paper towel at the bottom of the ramp to catch any water that runs down and off the leaves. Slowly, start pouring a little bit of water at the top of the ramp. Pour it in the middle, between the rulers, so that the trough will keep the water from spilling over the sides. If the leaves are waterproof, the water will run down the leaves and the paper towel placed underneath the ramp will stay dry.

What happened? Are the leaves waterproof?

Something more

A tree's leaves act like an umbrella. After a rain shower, look at or feel the ground under a tree and out in the open. Is it drier under the tree? That means it could be a good place to stand to stay dry during a rain shower. But never stand under a tree during a thunderstorm. It is a very dangerous thing to do, because the tree could be hit by lightning.

Look at the bottoms of the leaves. Are they dry? Do pine needles float? If so, they may be waterproof.

Project 142
STILL POLLUTED!
Discovering invisible pollution

We use so much water every day that we often forget just how important it is to us. Make a list of all the things water is used for around your house. Without water, we would not be able to live.

You need
- 2 small drinking glasses
- pepper
- paper coffee filter

Because water is so important, we must keep our sources of water clean. Once water is polluted, or dirty, it is often hard to make it clean again. Sprinkle about ten shakes of pepper from a pepper shaker into a small glass of water. Let it sit for two or three minutes. Put a paper coffee filter over the top of an empty drinking glass. Slowly, pour the pepper-polluted water through the filter and into the glass. Did the filter remove all of the black pieces of pepper? Does the water look clear again? Even if the water looks clear, maybe the filter did not really get rid of all the pepper pollution.

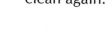

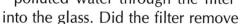

Taste the water. Does it still taste like pepper even though you can't see any?

Something more
Pollute clean water with other types of foods, like salt, and then use a filter to try to make the water clean again.

Project 143
SMELL POLLUTION
When unwanted odors stay in the air

Air pollution can mean unpleasant smells in the air. Some foods have unpleasant smells.

Have an adult cut a slice of fresh onion and place it on a dinner plate. Hold it up to your nose. Is the strong smell unpleasant? Does it make your eyes water?

Pour a capful of lemon juice over the slice of onion, completely covering it. Hold the slice up to your nose again. Is the onion smell as strong? Do your eyes still water?

If lemon juice takes away the unpleasant odor of onion, do you think it would be a good idea to add lemon juice to recipes that have onions in them, like tuna-fish salad?

Something more
Do other citrus fruit juices also take away strong food smells? Try pouring orange juice on a piece of fresh garlic.

> **You need**
> * fresh onion
> * a dinner plate
> * lemon juice
> * an adult with a kitchen knife

If you eat a piece of garlic, will drinking orange juice make your breath smell better?

Project 144
PLANT STRAWS
These roots are made for drinking

Some plants and trees have many little roots. Others have one larger, long root going deep into the ground. But add up the "sucking" area of the small roots, with all their tiny parts, called "root hairs," and you can understand how this root gathers more water faster than a larger root: its "surface area" is so much bigger. When it rains, the hairy root can quickly take in the water the plant or tree needs to live, before the rain soaks too far down into the soil. Having more root surface area makes it easier for plants to catch available water.

You need
- a piece of cotton clothesline
- 2 small, baby-food jars
- water

Discover how much more water a lot of small roots can gather, compared to one large root. Take one end of a piece of cotton clothesline. (Have an adult cut a piece for you.) Unravel and spread out about two inches (5 cm) of the clothesline, until all of the threads are separated. Fill two small jars half-full of water. (Be sure the jars are exactly alike and filled with the same amount of water.) Dip the end of the clothesline with the loose strands into one of the jars. Let the strands just touch the bottom of the jar. Hold it there and count to ten. Then pull the clothesline out. Take the other end of the clothesline, with the strands still wrapped tightly together. Dip that end into the other jar until it just touches the bottom. Hold it there and count to ten. Then pull the clothesline out.

Compare how much water is left in each of the jars. Did the end of the clothesline with more individual "roots" gather more water than the "single root" end?

Something more
Look at the root systems of different kinds of plants or vegetables. Identify the plants and write down which kind of root systems they have.

Project 145
RUNNING HOT & COLD
Testing air and soil as insulators

Many living things find shelter in the ground from hot and cold temperatures. Some animals sleep in the ground during the cold winter months. The ground protects plant bulbs and root systems from cold temperatures.

Fill two small soup cans with warm water from a sink. Put a thermometer in each can. Place one of the small cans in the middle of a bigger can. Fill the space in between the two cans with soil.

Place the other small can inside a bigger can, too, but don't put anything in between the two cans for insulation.

Write down the temperature showing on the thermometers. Every five minutes, look at the thermometers and write down the temperatures. Do this for a half hour.

Make a graph showing the rate of temperature change. Did the can of water surrounded by soil keep its heat longer than the one surrounded by air? Is soil a better insulator than air?

Something more
Is the best heat insulator also the best cooling insulator? Try other kinds of insulation, such as water or leaves.

You need
- 2 small soup cans
- 2 large cans about 5 inches (13 cm) in diameter
- 2 thermometers
- soil from your yard
- warm water
- a watch or clock
- pencil and paper

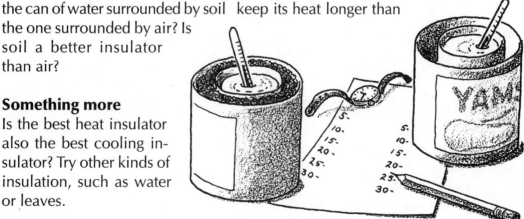

Project 146
HOLE IN THE SOIL
Comparing ground temperatures under trees

Deciduous trees are trees that lose all their leaves in the fall. An oak tree is one kind of deciduous tree. Conifers are trees that stay green all year. A pine tree is one kind of conifer. During the winter, is the ground underneath a pine tree warmer than the ground underneath an oak tree?

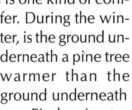

Find a pine tree and an oak tree in your yard, at your school, or in a neighborhood park. Underneath each tree, about two feet (60 cm) from the trunk, push a pencil or narrow stick into the ground to make a hole several inches deep. Put a thermometer into each hole. Wait a few minutes before reading the temperatures. What is the temperature under the pine tree? What is the temperature in the ground underneath the oak tree? What is the air temperature? Does it make a difference if the day is sunny or cloudy? What does the ground look like around each tree? Are there leaves piled around the oak tree?

You need
- oak tree
- pine tree
- 2 thermometers
- a cold winter day
- pencil and paper

Something more
Do the needles of a pine tree make a better blanket against cold than leaves? How would you go about setting up a project to test this guess, or hypothesis?

Are fruit trees any different?

Project 147
SCREENED INSECTS
Collecting and identifying neighborhood insects

What kinds of insects live in your neighborhood? Collect insects from windowsills around your home. An undisturbed screened window in an attic, garage, or shed, where insects are often trapped, may have a lot of dead insects gathered there. (Remember, spiders are arachnids, not insects. Insects have three pairs of legs, but arachnids have eight legs.)

You need
- dead insects
- a book on insects
- pencil and paper

Collect as many insects as you can find and identify them. You may want to mount the insects on a display board, and provide labels giving their name and something about them.

Quantify the number and types of insects you found. In other words, how many different kinds of dead insects did you find on the windowsills? Were there many more of one kind of insect than another?

Something more

Were any of the insects trapped on the windowsills still alive? Are the living insects helpful or harmful?

Project 148
GET A GRIP
Comparing the wraps that keep food fresh

We have many ways to preserve food, that is, to keep it fresh. After dinner, when there are leftovers, people often wrap them in plastic wrap, or put the food in bowls and cover them with the wrap.

If a plastic wrap is going to keep air out so that it will keep the food fresh, it must be able to cling well when it is wrapped around food (clings to itself) or over the top of a bowl (clings to bowl). Is there a "cling" difference in the brands of plastic food-wrap? Do some wraps cling better than others? Do a test and use science to help you be a better consumer.

Cut two pieces of a brand of plastic food-wrap. Each piece should measure one foot (30 cm) long by one foot wide. Use masking tape to attach one piece of the wrap to the edge of a table, so that it hangs down. Take the second piece of wrap and press it onto the bottom of the hanging piece, overlapping the pieces by two inches (5 cm).

You need
- 4 brands of plastic food-wrap
- a ruler
- masking tape
- spring-type clothes-pins
- scissors
- a table
- pencil and paper

Hang a spring-type clothespin on the bottom piece of wrap. Keep hanging more clothespins until the bottom piece of wrap falls off. Write down the number of clothespins the wrap held before it lost its grip.

Do this again for other brands of plastic wrap; include a store or generic (no-name) brand. Which food-wrap tested had the most cling? Which one had the least?

220

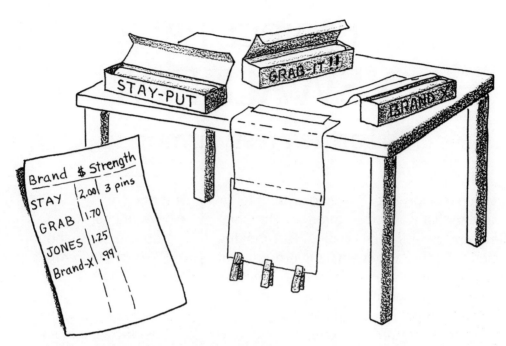

Compare the prices of the food-wrap you tested. Does the wrap that clings best also cost the most?

Which brands of wrap are the easiest and the hardest to get off the roll?

Something more

What about bowl cling? Put some coins or small stones into a bowl and cover it with the plastic wrap. Does it hold when you turn the bowl upside down? Watch out! Does the kind of bowl make a difference; that is, if it is made of plastic or glass? Does it matter if the outside of the bowl is wet or dry?

Do all brands of plastic wrap do a good job of keeping foods fresh? Cut five slices of apple. Wrap four of them in different brands of wrap. Mark them so you know which wrap is which. Leave one slice of apple unwrapped. Put them all in the refrigerator. Look at the slices every day. What do the apple slices look like at the end of a week?

Project 149
A SWALE DAY

Earth's grassy armor

A swale is a low area covered with grass or plant life that water runs through. The plant life keeps the soil from eroding. Fast-moving water can cause very damaging erosion, but the roots of grasses and plants help keep soil from being washed away. Prove that the roots of plants can help stop soil erosion.

Pour three measuring cups of water into a large pitcher. Fill a cookie tray with soil. There should be enough soil in the cookie tray so that it is as high as the tray's lip. Raise one end of the tray by piling several books under it. The raised end should be about 4 inches (10 cm) high. Put an-

You need
- large pitcher
- 4 cookie trays, about 18 inches (45 cm) wide
- soil
- a piece of soil with grass growing in it to fit in tray
- kitchen measuring cup
- water
- several thick books
- garden hand shovel

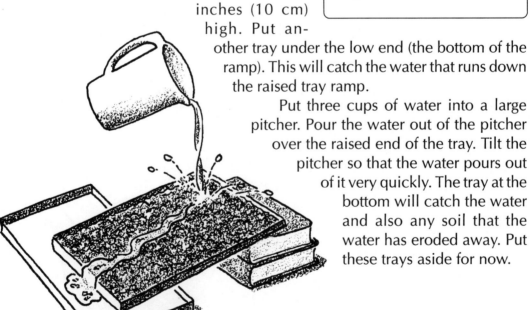

other tray under the low end (the bottom of the ramp). This will catch the water that runs down the raised tray ramp.

Put three cups of water into a large pitcher. Pour the water out of the pitcher over the raised end of the tray. Tilt the pitcher so that the water pours out of it very quickly. The tray at the bottom will catch the water and also any soil that the water has eroded away. Put these trays aside for now.

Get permission to take a piece of soil with grass growing on it from your yard or from an area in the neighborhood. Use a small garden hand shovel to cut a piece of soil large enough to fit a cookie tray. The piece should be about 2 inches (5 cm) deep to be sure to get the grass roots. Put the soil piece into

a cookie tray, being careful to keep it all together in one piece. Put books under one end of the tray to raise it to the same height as the other raised tray. At the low end, slide another empty cookie tray under it. Pour three cups of water into the pitcher. Pour the water out over the raised end of the tray. Tilt the pitcher the same as you did before, so that the water comes out very quickly. The tray at the bottom will catch the water and any eroded soil.

Look at the two trays that collected the water that ran off. Does one have more soil particles in it than the other one? Which one has more? Did the piece of soil with grass growing in it keep more of its soil than the other one?

As soon as the experiment is finished, put the piece of grass soil back in the ground where you found it so that the roots will catch and the grass will continue to grow.

Something more

Evaporate the water out of the two collecting trays. Weigh the soil that is left in each one and write down their weights.

Project 150
MUD HUTS

How to make a heat-retaining adobe brick

Many people live in houses made of wood. In the southwestern United States and in Mexico, where there are not many trees, people often build houses out of mud bricks called adobe. Even the ancient Babylonians and Egyptians, who lived in treeless desert areas, used adobe bricks. These bricks were made from sandy clay, water, and straw. They would bake the bricks in the sun for several weeks, and then use the dried, "cured" bricks to build their houses.

Adobe houses are warm in the evening and cool in the daytime. If a mud brick is warmed by the sun, how long will it continue to give off warmth once the sun goes down?

Gather some straw. (If you do not have straw you can use dry grass, or dry needles from under a pine tree.)

Put the straw, soil from your yard, and water into a bowl and mix it well. Open the top of an empty one-pint milk carton. Pour the mud mixture from the bowl into the milk carton. Make a hole in the mud by pushing a pencil halfway down in the middle of the opening. Loosen the mud around the pencil by moving the pencil in a small circle, then leave it in the carton. Put the milk carton in a sunny window and leave it there for several days to dry.

You need
- soil
- water
- bowl
- large mixing spoon
- straw or dry grass
- 2 thermometers
- one-pint milk carton
- clock
- a sunny window
- pencil and paper

When the brick is firm and dry, take the pencil out of it and peel off the carton. Leave your brick in a sunny window for one more hour. Then, put the brick on a table out of the sunlight.

Put a thermometer into the hole in the brick. This will measure the temperature inside the brick. Lay another thermometer nearby on the table to measure the temperature of the air outside the brick. Will the thermometer inside the brick measure a hotter temperature than the one outside the brick? Wait a few minutes, then read and write down the temperatures showing on the thermometer inside and outside of the brick. How long will it take before the thermometer inside the brick is the same temperature as the one outside of it?

Something more

Adobe bricks are not used for building in places where there is a lot of rain, or where it is cold. What do you think would happen if adobe bricks froze and thawed a lot? What happens to adobe bricks if they keep getting wet?

What could be added to the mud mix to make stronger bricks? Build a scale-model town out of adobe.

Project 151
A HOT LUNCH
Pets choose between heated or cooled foods

People eat foods at different temperatures. We eat cold ice-cream, room-temperature pea-nut-butter-and-jelly sandwiches, and hot ham-burgers. Pet cats and dogs usually eat their food at room temperature. Would they eat their food if it was cold? Would they eat it if it was hot? Do they like their food more if it is heated or cooled? What do you think your pet will like?

Put a small amount of pet food in three bowls. Cover each bowl with plastic food-wrap. Put one bowl of food in a warm sunny window. Put another bowl in the refrigerator. Put the third bowl on a table that is out of direct sunlight. After about an hour, take the plastic wrap off the bowls and put all three down where your pet usually goes for food. Watch your pet. What is its reaction to the three bowls. From which bowl does your pet eat? Does it eat from more than one bowl?

Something more
Does heat produce a stronger food smell? If so, maybe it is the stronger smell from the warm food that attracts your pet, rather than the temperature of the food. How could you find out if this is true?

Do cats and dogs react the same to different-temperature foods? Do some cats and some dogs react differently, really prefer hot or cold food?

Project 152
TRAPPED RAYS
Plastic food-wrap as an insulator

Is plastic wrap good to keep in warmth? Fill two small, plastic butter or margarine tubs with soil. Add water to the soil and mix to make mud. Push a thermometer into the middle of each tub of mud. Set both tubs in a warm, sunny window for one hour.

You need
- 2 small, plastic butter or margarine tubs
- plastic food-wrap
- 2 thermometers
- soil
- water
- spoon
- sunny window
- pencil and paper

An hour later, take the tubs out of the sunlight. Read the temperature showing on each thermometer, write it down (the temperatures should be the same), and put the thermometer back. Cover one of the tubs with some plastic wrap, wrapping it tightly around the thermometer. With the pencil, make a small hole (for the thermometer) through two or three more sheets of wrap. Place these over the wrapped tub, too. Be sure the plastic film is wrapped tightly around the whole tub.

Every fifteen minutes, look at the thermometers and record their temperatures. How long does it take for the two tubs of mud to lose their heat and reach room temperature? Did the tub covered with plastic wrap keep its warmth longer?

Something more

Do the experiment again, but this time cover one tub with one sheet of plastic wrap, and cover the other tub with two sheets. Does the tub wrapped with two sheets of wrap keep its warmth longer?

Test the ability of other things to keep heat in, like aluminum foil or paper napkins. What is the best insulator you can find?

Project 153
TREES, PLEASE

Wind protection for your home

Trees seem friendly. They are colorful and nice to look at. People hang swings from them. Birds build nests in them.

In places where the winters are cold, strong winds can make it harder to heat a house. Do trees stop the wind? If trees are planted around a house, can they help make it easier to heat the house?

On a windy day, go with an adult to an open place away from buildings and trees. Put a stone or small rock on the ground.

Take a plastic-foam drinking cup and, with your fingers, break off four small pieces. Hold one piece in your hand. Raise it in front of you as high as you can reach above the rock on the ground. Be sure you are standing so that your body is not blocking the wind. Let go of the piece. Mark the spot where it first hits the ground. Use a measuring stick or steel ruler to see how far the wind blew the plastic-foam piece away from the rock.

You need
• a place with many trees
• an open space, away from trees and buildings
• an adult
• plastic-foam drinking cup
• measuring stick or steel rule
• a windy day
• stone or small rock
• pencil and paper

Write down the distance. If it is a very windy day, the piece of the cup may blow too far. If that happens, use something a little heavier to drop, like a small piece of cloth. The cloth can be wet a little to make it even heavier, if needed.

Do this test again three more times. Each time, use a different piece of plastic foam or cloth to drop. Measure and write down the distances from the rock to the piece.

Add the four distances together, then divide the answer by four. This gives you the average distance the wind blew the pieces.

Pick up all the plastic-foam or cloth pieces and the rock when you leave. Do not litter.

Next, find a group of trees. The trees must have branches that go all the way to the ground, or there must be many bushes or shrubs surrounding the trees. Put the rock on the ground close to the trees. Again, standing by the rock, raise your hand in front of you as high as you can reach and let go of the piece of plastic foam. Measure how far away the wind blows the piece from the rock. Write down the distance.

Do this again three more times. Use a different piece of the foam cup each time. Measure and write down the distances from the rock to the piece of cup.

Add the four distances together. Divide the answer by four to get the average distance the wind blew the pieces.

The stronger the wind, the farther away the pieces of plastic foam will be carried. Which average distance was larger, the pieces dropped in the open space, or near the trees? What does this mean?

Something more

On which side of your house should you plant trees and shrubs to help protect your home from the winter winds (north, south, east, west)?

On which side of your house should you plant trees and shrubs to help protect it from the hot summer sun (north, south, east, west)?

Why do you think farmers might want to use trees to stop the wind?

Project 154
"CHEEPER" FOOD

Do birds prefer
popped or unpopped corn?

Birds like to eat seeds. Popped popcorn is a delicious treat for people, but corn is not found that way in nature. Bread is not found in nature either, but birds like it. What do you think birds would like best to eat, unpopped popcorn or popped popcorn?

Glue two small, plastic margarine or butter tubs near one edge of a stiff piece of cardboard The cardboard should be about the size of a sheet of typing paper. Fill one tub with unpopped popcorn and the other tub with popped popcorn. The popcorn should be plain, without butter. Put the cardboard on a windowsill with the tubs on the outside. To hold it and keep the wind from blowing it away, close the window on the cardboard. Now watch to see if any birds come to eat at the windowsill. Do they eat the popped corn, or the unpopped corn?

If no birds come to look at the popcorn, put a little birdseed or bread on the cardboard. This will be the bait, to attract them to your windowsill, then wait to see if they eat any of the popcorn from the tubs.

You need
- 2 small, plastic margarine or butter tubs
- stiff piece of cardboard
- glue
- popcorn
- a window

Something more
Identify the kinds of birds that come to your window. Pick up a book on birds at the library. Do some species of birds prefer the popped corn over the unpopped corn?

Try other kinds of "people food" to see if birds like them or not. You can serve breakfast cereals, fruits, vegetables, and liquids (soda, milk, juices).

Project 155
RIME OR REASON
Making water vapor visible

Did you ever go outside early in the morning and find the ground wet, even though it had not rained? That water all over the ground is dew.

In the air are tiny droplets of water. Most of the time these water droplets are hidden. They are too tiny to be seen. If there is a lot of water in the air, we see it as fog. But even when there is not enough water to make fog, some droplets are there. When the temperature of the air rises to a certain point, the water in the air cannot stay there. The temperature at which the water comes out of the air is called the dew point.

Is there water in the air in your room right now? Cold air can make the water vapor visible. Fill a plastic 1-litre soda bottle three-quarters full with water. Screw the cap on and place the bottle in the freezer. Wait until the water has turned to ice.

Take the bottle out of the freezer and set it on a dinner plate on a kitchen counter or table. The ice in the bottle will cool the air that comes near it. As the air cools, the hidden moisture in the air will appear on the outside of the bottle. Is white frost instead of water droplets forming on the bottle? That happens if the bottle is very cold. The white frost is called rime. It sometimes appears on window panes during very cold winter nights.

You need
- one-liter plastic soda bottle
- dinner plate
- kitchen table
- water
- use of a freezer
- pencil and paper

Something more
If the air coming out of your lungs is much warmer than the air around you, a cloud of moisture may be seen. Breathe on an eyeglass lens. What happens to the eyeglasses? What happens if the glasses are warmed first?

Project 156
MOISTURE, MOISTURE, EVERYWHERE
Testing humidity indoors and out

n the air all around us there are tiny droplets of moisture. We call this moisture that is in the air humidity. If there is a lot of moisture in the air we say that the humidity is high. When someone takes a hot shower, the room steams up. We can easily see that the humidity there in the bathroom is high.

Would you guess that the humidity in your home today is higher or lower than it is outside?

Cut two squares out of an old piece of cloth. Each piece should measure four inches (10 cm) square. Fold each piece in half, and then in half again.

Once you finish preparing the cloth, lay a pencil on a table. Set a ruler across the pencil, at about the middle so that it looks like a seesaw. Place one folded piece of cloth at one end of the ruler. Lay one thumbtack upside down on the cloth. Lay a second thumbtack upside down near the other end of the ruler. Move the pencil slowly under the ruler until it balances as well as possible.

Now, put another thumbtack upside down near the end of the ruler that does *not have* the piece of cloth on it; this will weight

You need
- 2 rulers
- 2 pieces of cloth, 4 inches (10 cm) square
- 6 thumbtacks
- 2 pencils
- safety scissors
- eyedropper
- paper
- clock or watch

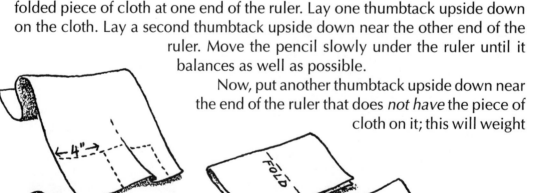

down that end. We now know that when the cloth is dry, the other end of the ruler will be heavier.

Fill an eyedropper with water. Slowly squeeze drops of water onto the cloth until the ruler tips and the water-soaked cloth side is now the heavier side. Be sure to count the number of drops you squeeze. Look at a clock or watch and write down the time. Keep checking the ruler balance. When the side of the ruler with the two thumbtacks touches the table, write down the time again. How long did it take for most of the moisture to dry out of the cloth?

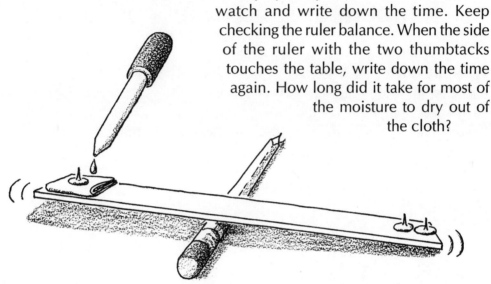

Make another seesaw ruler, just like this one, outside. Squeeze the same number of water drops onto the cloth as you did inside. Write down the time and keep checking the balance. When the side of the ruler with the two thumbtacks touches the table, write down the time. If the air inside is dryer than the air outside, the water on the cloth in the house will evaporate and the cloth will dry quicker than the water on the cloth outside.

Did you guess right?

Something more

Is there any difference in the humidity of the air outside on a sunny day compared to on a cloudy day?

Is there any difference in the humidity of the air during the day compared to at night?

Project 157
UPDRAFT
Temperature and water convection

When a body of air becomes warmer than the other air around it, that body of air rises. It rises because it is lighter and less dense than the other air. Warm air rises and cold air falls. When air moves this way, it is called convection. On a hot summer day, you can see warm air rising from a blacktop road or from a barbecue grill.

Convection happens with water, too. When you go swimming at a lake, you may notice that the water by your feet, when you are standing, feels colder than the water at your chest. During the day, the water in the lake or pond is warmed by the sun hitting the surface. During the night, the water on the surface cools off first. As it does, the water drops down. The warmer water underneath is then pushed up, because cold water is heavier and more dense than warm water.

To prove that this hypothesis is true, pour water into a clear drinking glass. Put the glass of water in the refrigerator. Also, put in the refrigerator a bottle of blue food coloring. Wait one hour, and then take them both out of the refrigerator

Fill the other clear drinking glass with hot water from a sink faucet. Do not make it too hot: you don't want to burn yourself.

> **You need**
> - 2 clear drinking glasses
> - water
> - bottle of red food coloring
> - bottle of blue food coloring
> - use of a refrigerator
> - spoon

With the bottle of red food coloring at room temperature, slowly squeeze six drops into the glass of cold water. Because the cold water is denser, the red coloring stays on top. Slowly squeeze six drops of red food coloring into the glass of hot water. What happens?

Stir both glasses. Then, squeeze six drops of the cold, blue food coloring into the glass of cold water. What happens? Squeeze six drops of the blue food coloring into the glass of hot water. Does the blue coloring sink?

Something more

Instead of using food coloring in the two glasses of water in this project, can you find natural food coloring to use? Try juice from a can of red beets, a weak tea, or some cranberry juice.

Project 158
BAG RECYCLING
Uses for brown paper grocery bags

We must be careful with the things we have. Conservation is using things wisely and not wastefully. If you want to conserve, buy only things that can be used again and again. When cleaning, use reusable rags instead of paper towels. Use regular dishes and glasses for meals, instead of paper plates and throwaway cups.

You need
• paper grocery bags
• glue
• safety scissors
• a heavy book
• large jar lid
• pencil

In addition to using things more than once, you also conserve by using things for more than one purpose. The paper bags that you get from food stores when they pack your groceries can be re-used by making them into coasters (the small mats that go under a drinking glass or cup to protect a tabletop).

Lay a paper bag flat on a table. Place a large jar lid on the bag. Use a pencil to trace the outside circle of the lid onto the bag. The coaster must be bigger around than the drinking glass, so check to see that the size will fit the glasses used in your home.

Cut out the circle with scissors. Use the lid again to trace four more circles on the paper bag. Cut them out. Place some glue around the edges of the circles and stick them together, one on top of the other like a layer cake. Be neat. Do not use too much glue, or it will seep out. Place a heavy book on top of the stack of paper circles and wait until the glue dries.

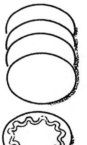

236

Cut enough circles (or squares) to make a set of four or five coasters. Decorate the tops with pictures cut from magazines or comic books. The finished coasters can be given as gifts. You could decorate a set of coasters with cancelled postage stamps and give it to a friend who collects stamps.

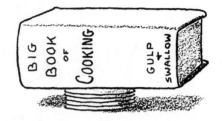

How good are your paper coasters at keeping a table dry if a very cold drink, with ice cubes, is placed on them? Are five layers of paper enough to keep the table dry? If not, how many layers are needed?

What if you put wax paper or aluminum foil circles in between the paper circles?

Something more

You probably have lots of paper grocery bags. What other uses can you think of for them? Why not use them to make paper dolls, cutouts, puppets, masks, and book covers for school?

When you go grocery shopping, take some paper or plastic bags back with you to pack your groceries at the checkout, so you won't have to use new ones.

Project 159
WHO'S RAPPING, TAPPING?

Determining sound direction

You need
- 7 friends
- 14 pencils
- a blindfold
- a large bowl
- safety scissors
- paper

We have five senses to learn about our environment. Our ears are the wonderful organs that let us hear sounds. Because our ears are placed one on either side of our head (instead of both on the same side), our brain can figure out from the signals where a sound is coming from. Using your two ears, can you find your friends from the tapping sounds they make?

With scissors, cut seven small pieces of paper. Write a number on each piece, from 1 to 7. Put all the pieces of paper in a large bowl.

Gather seven friends. Give each person two pencils. Tell your friends to each pick a piece of paper from the bowl. Give one person a sheet of paper. That person will keep count of how many guesses you get right.

Stand in the middle of a room and have a friend blindfold you. Tell your friends to stand in a big circle around you, with you in the middle. One by one, have each friend tap two pencils together three times. The friend who picked the paper marked "1" goes first. After your friend taps the pencils together, point to where you think the sound is coming from. The person who is keeping track of whether your guesses are right or wrong writes it down each time you point.

After the first person has tapped the pencils together and you have made your guess, the friend who has the paper numbered "2" should tap his or her pencils together three times. Again, point to where you think the sound is coming from. Have each friend take a turn as you make your guesses, until all seven have gone.

How many did you get right?

Something more

How far apart in distance do two sounds have to be before you can tell that they are coming from two different places? Have two friends stand close to each other and take turns tapping their pencils. Explain that sometimes the same person should take two turns, to see if you can tell that the sound has not moved.

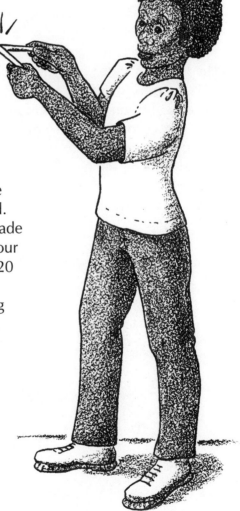

Try to tell the difference in a sound made about two feet (60 cm) below and above your ear when your friend is standing four feet (120 cm) in back of you?

Cover one ear and then try the tapping experiment with your seven friends again. How many do you think you will get right using only one ear compared to when you use both ears? What if you turn your head between taps?

Project 160
STAR BIG, STAR BRIGHT

Sizing up our sun

The diameter of an object is a measure of how big it is through its center. Even though the sun is very far away, it is so large (its diameter is about 865,000 miles or 1,393,000 kilometres across) that the sun sends us its star light in a wide path. The light even seems to be coming to us from more than one place, because the sun can make more than one shadow of things.

You need
- ruler
- sheet of white paper
- pencil
- a sunny day

On a sunny day, put a piece of white paper on the ground outside and lay a pencil on it. Then pick up and hold the pencil about a foot (30 cm) above the paper. Do you see two shadows of the pencil? Slowly move the pencil down towards the ground until you see only one shadow. With a ruler, measure how far from the ground the pencil has to be before only one shadow is visible.

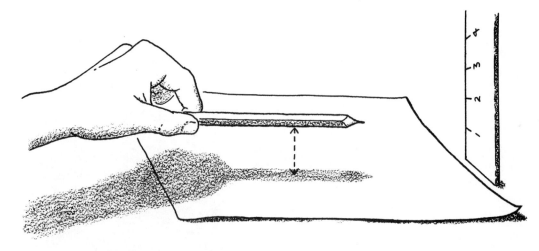

Something more

When air is heated to different temperatures, what we see through it seems to shake. Sometimes, on a hot summer day, if you look far away and close to the ground, you will see things shaking because of this heated air. The same thing happens if you look at something across the top of a hot stove. The object will look as if it is shaking.

Air heated to different temperatures is what makes the stars in the night sky seem to shake, or twinkle. Because the planets are much closer to us than the faraway stars, they look larger and more light from them reaches our eyes, so the planets we see do not twinkle. The light from the planets is not really their own, but is light reflected from the sun. An astronomy book from the library can help you identify what you see in the night sky. At many times during the year you can see the planets Venus and Mars by using only your eyes. Can you see that the stars twinkle and the planets do not?

GLOSSARY

adobe A mixture of clay, water, and either straw or pine needles made into bricks and baked in the sun. For thousands of years, people living in desert areas, such as the ancient Babylonians and Egyptians, Mexicans, and Indians in the southwestern United States, made their houses out of adobe bricks.

assumption When doing a science experiment, scientists often make assumptions that certain things are true. An assumption is something that is believed to be true. In Project 1 of this book, a glass of a light-colored soda and a glass of a dark-colored soda are used to find in which glass an ice cube will last longest if the glasses are placed in sunlight. The experiment is to learn the difference caused by sunlight on color, but it assumes that the differing contents of the dark and the light sodas (fruit juice, carbonation, sugar, and sugar replacement) have no effect on the melting of the ice cube.

asteroid A small planetoid or chunk of rock revolving around the sun; most travel between the orbits of Mars and Jupiter. Asteroids that stray in our direction may become meteors.

atom The smallest unit of an element.

axis A straight line on which an object turns. The imaginary line from the North to the South Pole is the Earth's axis. Plural is axes.

calories For the human body to function, it needs energy. We get energy for our bodies by eating foods. The amount of energy we can get from a particular food is measured in units called calories.

capacitor An electronic component used in television sets, computers, radios, and other electronic devices, which performs a variety of tasks. Capacitors can temporarily store electrical charges.

center of gravity The point at which the total weight of an object balances.

centrifugal force A force that pushes outward when an object is moving in a curve.

chaos A confused, unorganized condition.

characteristic Whatever is different or special about something, so that it can be described.

classification A method of grouping things based on what is the same about them and their characteristics.

comet A packed collection of gas, dust and ice crystals that move around the sun in orbits that take them outside the solar system.

compost pile All kinds of decomposing material that makes soil nutritious to plants.

coniferous tree A tree that bears cones, such as a pine tree. Trees that stay green all year are called "evergreens." See also deciduous tree.

constellation An observed pattern of stars, used to help locate and identify individual stars and other celestial bodies, such as the Northern Hemisphere's constellation Orion.

consumers Those who use up, or consume, things in their environment. It is important to be a wise consumer.
control group A group that is left alone. The experimental group is later compared to the "left alone" group to see if there are any differences.

convection The movement of a liquid or a gas caused by temperature. Hot air rises and cold air falls. Cold water falls when placed in hot water.

deciduous tree A tree that loses its leaves in the fall, as opposed to those trees known as "evergreens." An oak tree is one kind of deciduous tree.

decompose The breaking down of something into simpler molecules.

density How tightly packed together the molecules of a substance are. Water is denser than wood, so wood floats in water.

diameter A measurement straight through the center of an object from one edge to the other. The diameter of the sun, for example, measures about 865,000 miles or 393,000

drag An aviation term for the resistance of air to the forward motion of an aircraft. The drag force tries to slow the plane down the faster it moves through the air.

eclipse When one body blocks out the light from a more distant body.

element A basic building block from which everything in the universe is made.

environment Everything in the world around us: including air, water, soil, trees, sounds, smells, buildings, furniture.

equator An imaginary circle that is midway between the north and south poles of a sphere.

equinox A time of the year during the Earth's movement around the sun when the North and South Poles are equally distant from the sun. The vernal equinox occurs in the spring. The autumnal equinox occurs in the fall.

erosion A wearing away of soil or other matter, usually by wind or water.

evaporation The process that changes a liquid into a gas.

experiment An activity done to prove whether a hypothesis, or guess, is true or false.

fluorescent bulb (see "incandescent bulb")

frequency With regard to radio waves, the "frequency" of an electromagnetic wave is the number of times it "vibrates," or "cycles," per second.

friction The resistance to motion when two things rub together. Rub your hands together briskly and friction will cause you to feel warmth. Sometimes friction is desirable, such as when you are trying to walk on ice. Melting ice reduces friction, making ice very slippery!

germination The time between when a seed begins to sprout a root and a leaf (using its own stored energy) and when it is able to make food on its own

gravity A force of attraction between two objects.

Hubble Space Telescope A sensitive telescope orbiting the Earth. It lets astronomers study the stars without having to look through the Earth's atmosphere, which can make it hard to see and cause distortion.

humidity The amount of water vapor there is in the air. Humidity can be high (a lot of moisture) or low (not much moisture).

hypothesis A thoughtful, reasoned guess about something, based on what is known. A hypothesis must be proven by experimentation.

incandescent bulb The most common types of electric lights used in our homes are incandescent and fluorescent bulbs. In both kinds of light, electrical energy is turned into light energy. In an incandescent light bulb, electricity passes through a small wire, called a filament, which glows brightly. In a fluorescent light bulb (which is often in the shape of a long, straight tube or a circular tube), the inside of the bulb is filled with a gas. The inside glass of the bulb is coated with materials called phosphors. When electricity is passed through a heating element in the bulb, the gas gives off rays, which cause the phosphors to fluoresce (glow).

insulator A substance used to keep something at its current temperature, lowering the effect of a different outside temperature.

kilowatt-hour A unit of measure of electrical power consumption used by power companies in determining how much to charge their customers for the electricity they use. A kilowatt is 1,000 watts. It takes one kilowatt-hour of electrical energy to operate ten 100-watt light bulbs for one hour.

latitude/longitude Angular distances on a globe: parallel, or lateral, to the equator is called latitude; lengthwise, from a designated zero-degree meridian, is longitude.

LED (light emitting diode) An electronic component that produces a small light from a semiconductor material. LED's are commonly used in watches and as light indicators on home stereos, computers, and other home electronic appliances.

light pollution The brightness of light other than the light from the stars, which spoils your view of the night sky.

light-year Not a measure of time; a light-year measures the distance light travels through space in a year, about 5.9 trillion miles (9.5 trillion kilometers). Not counting our own sun, a star that is only eight light-minutes away, it takes the light from Proxima Centauri, our closest star, 4.2 light-years to reach us.

litmus paper Paper treated to change color depending on the amount of acid or alkaline (measure of pH) in a liquid.

magnetism A force recognized by the ability of certain objects to attract iron.

magnitude A standard measurement of the brightness of stars.

mass The density of "stuff" packed into an object. The more mass something has, the heavier it is. A Ping-Pong ball and a golf ball are about the same size and shape, but a golf ball has more mass.

meteor, meteoroid, meteorite Chunks of debris traveling through space are called meteoroids. When a meteoroid enters the Earth's atmosphere it is called a meteor. Most meteors burn up completely from friction in the Earth's atmosphere, but when one hits the ground it is called a meteorite. Meteor Crater in Arizona is believed to be the impact site of a long-ago meteor strike.

microfarad A unit of measure of electrical storage used to indicate how much of an electric charge can be stored by an electrical component called a capacitor

microwaves A kind of radio frequency energy. They are electromagnetic waves. Their frequency (the number of times the wave vibrates each second) is much higher than most other types of radio and TV waves. Microwaves are used for telephone and satellite communications as well as for cooking in "microwave ovens."

migration Moving from one area to another. Birds and animals usually migrate because of the change of seasons or to look for food.

moisture Tiny droplets of water vapor in the air or that form on something because of condensation. Also, water in any form.

molecule The smallest unit of something; much too small to be seen with the naked eye. Molecules are made up of even smaller atoms.

nocturnal Something more active at night, such as certain animals and plants.

nuclear energy A type of energy that is released when the nuclei of atoms are either combined together (called fusion) or split apart (called fission). The energy released, called "nuclear energy," is in the form of heat, light, or some other type of radiation. Nuclear energy is used to make electricity by heating steam that drives giant turbine generators.

observation Using your senses-smelling, touching, looking, listening and tasting-to study something closely, sometimes over a long period of time.

orbit The path an object takes around another celestial body.

particle A very tiny bit of something. When two chalk erasers are clapped together, particles of chalk can be seen in the air.

pH An acid/base scale used to show the alkalinity or acidity of a liquid.

photosynthesis The process of a plant making its food by gathering light energy from the sun is called photosynthesis. Also needed in the process are carbon dioxide, water, chlorophyll (which gives leaves their green color), and trace amounts of minerals.

planet A massive body that orbits a sun and shines by reflecting its light. Our solar system has nine major planets and many minor planets, or asteroids.

pollution Anything that is harmful to the environment.

radio frequency energy Electromagnetic waves used to carry TV and radio signals.

recycle To use something again and again. Some product packaging uses recycled materials.

rime Moisture from the air that forms as a white frost, such as on the inside of a window on very cold winter days.

roll One of the three axes of flight. An imaginary line can be drawn from the front of the plane out through the back (an axis). When the plane tilts on this axis, one wing becomes lower than the other does. The tilting movement along this axis is called roll.

room temperature The temperature at which most active people feel comfortable, usually about 68 to 70 degrees Fahrenheit (20-21 degrees C).

sample group A smaller group that takes the place of a much larger group, in order to do a test. The size of the sample group should be big enough to give a true picture of the larger group.

scientific method A step-by-step way of proving a hypothesis to be true or false.

star A very hot, glowing ball of gases. The sun is our closest star.

surface area The part of an object that is in contact with the outside.

tannic acid An acid found in tea and in some tree bark.

telescope From the Greek words tele, "from afar," and skopos, "viewer." An instrument that collects light and, with lenses, enables us to see faraway objects up close and with more detail. The Italian scientist Galileo Galilei, in 1608, was the first astronomer to use a telescope.

thermometer An instrument used to measure warmth.

trajectory The path of an object as it travels through the air.

twilight The part of the evening after the sun sets, when the Earth's atmosphere continues to reflect the sun's light. Twilight lasts for about an hour after the sun goes down.

waning/waxing Observed changes of the moon's phases. When the phase of the moon is between being completely dark (New Moon) and completely illuminated (Full Moon), it is said to be waxing, or building its way up to a Full Moon. When the phase of the moon is between a Full Moon and a New Moon, it is said to be waning, showing less and less light until it isn't lit at all. Then the cycle repeats.

wavelength Energy can travel in the form of a wave. You are familiar with rolling waves in the ocean. Other types of energy waves, such as sound waves and radio waves, would look similar to ocean waves, if we could see them. A wave has a "crest," or peak, the highest part of the wave, and it has a trough, the lowest part. The length from crest to crest (or trough to trough) is called the "wavelength." The wavelength of a tsunami (a tidal wave) can be 100 miles (161 kilometers) long! The wavelength of a 550 Hertz (cycles per second) sound wave, which is a note that is a little higher than "middle C" on a piano, is 2 feet.

windbreak An object that reduces the force of the wind. Trees are sometimes planted around a house to act as a windbreak, protecting the house from strong winds.

yaw One of the three axes of flight. An imaginary line (axis) can be drawn from the top of the plane out through the bottom. The plane can turn to one side or the other along this axis. This turning movement is called yaw.

INDEX